Entwined
Hearts

ENTWINED Hearts

The Sunset of Alzheimer's Disease
and More of Life's Realities

JJ JANICE

Copyright © 2023 by JJ Janice

ISBN: 978-1-77883-150-8 (Paperback)

All rights reserved. No part of this publication may be reproduced, distributed, or transmitted in any form or by any means, including photocopying, recording, or other electronic or mechanical methods, without the prior written permission of the publisher, except in the case brief quotations embodied in critical reviews and other noncommercial uses permitted by copyright law.

The views expressed in this book are solely those of the author and do not necessarily reflect the views of the publisher, and the publisher hereby disclaims any responsibility for them.

BookSide Press
877-741-8091
www.booksidepress.com
orders@booksidepress.com

To all those who walk the path of Alzheimer's disease—victims of memory loss and their families, caregivers, friends, neighbors, and strangers.

It includes people who have experienced the realities of bipolar disorder, alcoholism, drugs, incarceration, stress, and beyond.

May peace and love come to the many silent prayer warriors among us; all shall be remembered, and know you are not walking this path alone.

Contents

Preface ix

Acknowledgments xi

Introduction xiii

Chapter 1   Every Person Has Worth..1

Chapter 2   Good Homes Located..9

Chapter 3   The Book Comes Alive..17

Chapter 4   Guest Author Day..24

Chapter 5   Birthday Surprise 31

Chapter 6   The Good Life 37

Chapter 7   I've Been Waiting for You 48

Chapter 8   The Questions..54

Chapter 9   Asking for Help 60

Chapter 10 The Center...68

Chapter 11 Facing Reality..101

Chapter 12 Lynn 117

Chapter 13 Can't Handle Any More..132

Chapter 14   Marijuana and Alcoholism 142

Chapter 15   Fighting Bipolar Disorder 150

Chapter 16   Alzheimer's Disease and Health Concerns 154

Chapter 17   Everyone Is Human 158

Chapter 18   The Closing Doors 163

Resources 175

Preface

This is a work of nonfiction. Names, characters, businesses, places, and incidents are used in a fictitious manner. Any resemblance to actual persons, living or dead, or actual events is purely coincidental. The information in this book is meant to supplement but not replace a proper and thorough education regarding Alzheimer's and bipolar disorder, stress, drugs, and alcoholism. Please find a list of the author's personal findings used for resources in the back of this book.

Acknowledgments

Special thanks to my coworkers Laverne and Patty for challenging my experiences with Alzheimer's disease and stretching to help others who might feel they are all alone.

Also thanks to my Canadian friend, Judy, who encouraged me to write *Entwined Hearts*. This book is dedicated to her.

Thank you.

Introduction

Entwined Hearts is about a two-year experience with Alzheimer's disease that connected a mother, a daughter, and a common stranger. It started with an ESL/ELL class where the facilitator requested books. Eventually the connection between the author and facilitator advanced to a promise, and everyone took that promise seriously. Over time, the mother (author), daughter (bipolar disorder), and stranger (facilitator) were drawn close during the last stage of Alzheimer's.

Meeting these two ladies changed my life. I went from being timid to gaining self-confidence and advancing to standing up for those unable to represent themselves because of the poor choices they had made earlier in life. Combating life's hardships and learning how to forgive when deep hurts prevail have helped me to step out of my safe zone. Now it has become easier for me to take chances, speaking out about real-life attitudes hidden inside homes where the public eye is not allowed to hear or see the family's real life. It is vital to remember to say "I love you" and to keep a promise.

I have felt alone at times, and I have realized that people do not want to speak or listen to various topics except in therapy groups. It often seems taboo to ask about Alzheimer's disease, drugs, bipolar disorder, alcoholism, and incarceration, and how stress is handled in each of these circumstances, and these topics are usually met with quietness. Thus, I researched websites to advance my knowledge.

During the last several years, I kept a secret diary to compartmentalize my feelings and experiences. I often required high maintenance at times to accept what I had encountered in life. These moments affected people's future realities. Hopefully by reading *Entwined Hearts* people will realize that they are not alone in facing Alzheimer's disease, death, and other life experiences.

Chapter 1

Every Person Has Worth

Time flies by! Already it has been several years since my two special ladies left on their eternal vacation. The mother, Anita, had Alzheimer's and was not expected to live much longer. The daughter, Lynn, battled bipolar disorder, drugs, alcoholism, and even incarceration during her younger life. The choices people make in life on a daily basis affect everyone's future, not just the futures of those making the good or bad decisions. From these two ladies I learned that every person has self-worth and that it's important to keep a promise.

Over time I found that I needed to freely speak with someone who would not judge or question my experiences in my two-year relationship with this family. Our lifestyles were totally different in some ways yet very similar in some challenges. The mother and I enjoyed teaching, while the daughter and I lived life sometimes in our own bubbles we had created, afraid to step into reality. There was a fear to allow anyone to know who we really were as human beings. Yet all three of us had so much in common because we loved life.

I stepped forward and spoke with friends about my two-year experience. I felt their silent words. I imagined them saying things like "Get over it. You're not even blood family." However, something kept tugging at my open heart, especially in regard to the mother's words "I've been waiting for you." I realized that saying "I love you" must come from the heart.

I greatly appreciated my friends as each separately listened to my stories, and their honesty was refreshing. Their strong shoulders encouraged me to smile during extremely sad times when my heart was deeply crushed by these two ladies' lives and deaths. My friends' warm hearts and hugs carried my emotions so I didn't stumble and fall into depression.

However, I quickly learned that speaking with people wasn't a good idea, because my friends couldn't relate to my experiences, especially a promise from a stranger. Thus, after a considerable amount of time, the conclusion was simply to speak with a person who wasn't real. I thought about writing in a diary to log my various experiences. Then my mind changed back to an unreal person to write to. I could write freely to a person who wasn't real. Writing about my experiences with these two ladies now has become peaceful. They had such a positive impact on my future choices in life and taught me how important it is to face circumstances with a positive attitude.

My mind entertained that perhaps a psychologist would be good, but he or she would have had to take notes and ask questions—questions I didn't want to face because I just wanted someone to listen to me. I could speak freely in front of a person who wasn't real. I wondered how many other people needed to know they were not alone after they faced such hardships in life.

In today's world people use a keyboard to type words onto a blank screen. The information is kept silently in a computer. This form of communication would be my way of releasing frustrations and stress. I would write to someone who would not be judgmental or critical of my experiences. I needed to pour out my thoughts only to quiet listening ears. This fake person would be referred to as my dearest diary, and using my computer would be like using a pen. My dearest diary would become my closest friend. I would call myself the common stranger.

This was my right path. It would allow me to be free to pen my experiences and my heart's growing love for these two people, who were changing my life. Life is full of surprises, adventures, and predictions. Every day we make choices. I think about the true meaning of life and how it had been filled with loads of laughter during visits with Anita and Lynn. Our laughter helped release the deep stress involved with the circumstances of Alzheimer's and other issues.

I have looked at life differently since meeting these two people. Life will always include good and bad seasonal experiences. The good seasons are where prayers become special praises. It's like going for a walk and stopping to smell the roses. Praise God Almighty for bringing these two ladies into my life. It's those bad choices that make me feel defeated. The bad choices become cold like a snow blizzard in winter covering emotions. After these times I'm usually begging for forgiveness from God Almighty. It's all in keeping good attitudes and trusting faith.

As I expand in years, the seasonal experiences become more precious. There are so many wonderful people bringing laughter and joy into my heart like Anita and Lynn did. It's refreshing to be around happy people. They stimulate my energy so that I'm more positive. My friend Sue does that. Then there are seasons that bring people who disrupt my values like Lynn did. Are these values silent standards for how people live or what they stand up for? Perhaps it is more the honesty, integrity, and even the freedom that comes from a conscience, knowing right from wrong.

It has become very humbling knowing people really care about me as a human being during hard times. Realizing I am actually not alone and that others have been through these same or similar challenging times brings me hope for a positive future.

Over the past several years, there have been different types of seasons in my life. Each season presents various experiences. Lynn constantly moved around the world, whereas I grew up on a berry and chicken farm. She once said, "Growing up and living in various countries, we had servants." I cleaned my own room and helped with chores, weeding the berry fields preparing food for lunch and dinner, and doing the dishes. Both of us loved sports. Running often took away the daily built-up stresses. Neither one of us had lasting childhood friendships. But she told me her stories about how she kept making bad decisions into her adulthood. Fortunately, these types of choices seldom connected Lynn and me. In a way we both were loners who liked being associated with people but kept mostly to ourselves. Neither Lynn nor I liked to gossip.

While living abroad with her parents, Lynn's self-identity was positive, but it turned negative when the family relocated to central Texas during her late teenage years. She was a highly accomplished runner and swimmer in the schools she had attended in countries overseas. But it was hard adjusting to her new world in the United States, where she felt there was no place for her to showcase her talents. Even *almost* making the master's swim team made a difference in Lynn's future. Neither Lynn nor Anita forgot that devastating teenage experience. Who could this teenager talk with about her time living in different countries and knowing other cultures? Most other normal teens did not understand living in other parts of the world. Lynn had a secret desire to go to college and to work toward obtaining a PhD, but this deep desire was only fulfilled years later through a loving relative.

Later as a grown adult, Lynn learned to make better choices, but her past followed each path she took, including the times when she started looking for work. Lynn's early-adult life choices were very disappointing and heart-wrenching for her parents. Could they ever really forgive her?

Her mother dreamed of a better future for her child, but during those trying years, thoughts of creating a fictitious person crept into Anita's mind. Anita was deeply hurt by the way Lynn lived during her young adult years. Anita hid her sorrows as much as possible from relatives, friends, neighbors, and associates. Was Anita a priceless silent prayer warrior who could bring thoughts into reality because she was a writer? She was one very strong-willed woman with deep hurts. What did forgiveness mean between this mother and daughter?

Anita and Lynn spoke often about their lives in different ways, even their deaths. Anita was a dedicated wife and mother who wanted to die because she knew how Alzheimer's would steal her mind. She felt her life experiences were far too precious for this intruder.

Anita's Alzheimer's was little by little attacking different parts of her brain, taking away memories and experiences, even blanking out precious names of close family members, people, and circumstances. Alzheimer's thrives on moving memories into a dark, limitless void. Time was not on Anita's side.

Throughout Anita's life she knew the importance of education. She became a librarian, historian, traveler, and writer, but her family was always her number-one concern. She was connected in the community and highly respected. When Anita found out she had Alzheimer's, this mother asked her daughter, Lynn, to help her die, but Lynn also loved life and just could not assist with her mother's request.

Anita and I spoke about how important it was for this family's ties to continue to grow strong and close as they moved around the world. She would take a fake Christmas tree everywhere they moved to keep this tradition alive. Hearing the simple words "I love you" acted like glue, holding each family member's heart together. It's not easy moving in the service. Somehow these simple words were not always enough to cover forgiveness. Anita was very angry at Lynn because of her past life and how embarrassing it was to the family name. Meanwhile, Lynn felt she needed to prove her worthiness to her parents, showing everyone that her lifestyle had changed. She longed to be accepted by her parents.

It amazed me how easy it was for Anita to say to me, "I love you. I've been waiting for you," but why would she give such kind words to me yet yell at her own daughter? Would Lynn's mother ever speak these precious words to her daughter, who longed to hear them from her mother's own lips? My life was becoming entwined in their lives, and our hearts were bleeding together as I noticed deep hurts between mother and daughter.

Both Anita and Lynn had very high IQs. Anita believed she could conquer anything, including Alzheimer's. Lynn thought drugs could control circumstances. This common stranger became the missing piece to a lonely woman's life. I remember thinking about how God had quite a sense of humor, placing people together for His purposes. Or was this all accomplished through prayers?

What amazed me was that even with Alzheimer's, Anita and I could communicate. Once I asked Anita what her first words were when Lynn was born. "A little girl," replied Anita. How amazing! This lady in the last stage of Alzheimer's understood exactly what I was asking her. When I reported back to Lynn what her mother said, I added the word *beautiful*.

Lynn must have picked up on my editorializing because she dismissed the comment. She just said, "I wish Mom would tell me she loves me." Yes, my dearest diary, I did speak a little lie to Lynn, but I am still glad I did it. Perhaps it helped improve this mother-daughter relationship. I know God hates lying. Let Him be my judge.

My dearest diary, Lynn once told me (in front of her husband) that *she just knew* her mother wished she had aborted her. Was that really her truth? What a horrible comment to tell a daughter! Can a person know what is in another person's heart? Can a person look, listen, and read between the lines another person has spoken? It's between these two people. Each person must make his or her very own decision as to what life is worth. As for me, I choose life.

I've thought about this family and how difficult it must have been to constantly move around (since their family was in the service). I know there was significant closeness in this family. There must have been much forgiveness too.

I observed how this mother and daughter connected and disconnected. I saw the deep meaning of love in their attitudes along with their disagreements. And I've seen and heard stories of how deep hurts shattered the love at times. Anita knew her husband and children loved her, but she longed to be *remembered*. This was a family with so many hurts.

Growing mature during various seasons is essential to choosing and accepting our decisions. Nothing stands still. Either life moves forward, or one will live in the past. If a person lives in the past, always remembering the bad, then they lose the ability to move forward. Each of life's experiences is an opportunity to step forward into a higher, more positive, and happier life. The choice is exactly that—a choice. These seasons have become more and more precious as time has advanced my years. My choices are more thought out now, and my decisions have become very precious.

I learned something very interesting during those two years—creative mix-matches. Before meeting Anita and Lynn, I never related to the idea of creative reality. How could people create in their hearts (subconscious minds) the beginning of a reality? Now I know that through personal experience people can create in their hearts and minds what they want and desire. It's called hard work and finding a way to keep the dream alive and meeting a goal. It's a person's faith that will determine the forthcoming creation.

Positive creative thinking really works. If you think positive thoughts, there will be a positive force at work in your life. If you think negative thoughts there will be a negative force at work in your life. When people combine their positive creativity thoughts with their faith, it is at that point the desired positive thoughts will move beyond self-will. By speaking verbally what is in your heart, you can inspire deeply hidden desires to move toward existence. Joining words, pictures, and thoughts with faith can eventually bring things into reality. It just takes time to coordinate everything together. As for Anita, it took years to turn her ideal dream person into reality as she carved the image of a person. Everything and everyone connected must be on the same wavelength for everything to come together.

My dearest diary, time really does fly by quickly. My eyes watched Anita became very frail. Meanwhile, Lynn desired to become the family's matriarch. As for me, I am just a common stranger who learned I was worth my weight in gold by helping two deeply hurting family members.

Over time it became clear to me how Anita was a lonely woman who wanted to be *remembered*. While she was sick, each day was the same. Who would take time to visit with her? Her family, her books, her joys, and her sorrows were real. Did she have a memory bucket list? Was she checking off and able to let go of the past joys that were on her memory lists before she lost them to the black void of Alzheimer's?

Each of us three women viewed Alzheimer's and life differently. Lynn viewed me as someone who moved into her mother's life. She questioned my presence as her mother welcomed giving me her books. Over time Lynn appreciated me, the stranger. Eventually, Lynn became more aware of a closeness developing between her mother and me. This moved her mind to jealousy and then envy.

Meanwhile, Anita did not want to become helpless. She had been independent all of her life. She had always lived life to the fullest and made her own decisions. As for my life, it became more open, more flexible, and more caring about other people. I saw firsthand some of the mean realities this family went through as they watched their loved one's mind blackened out by Alzheimer's. How could they handle all of this stress under constantly difficult circumstances?

Hopefully, through time they will all heal from the deep hurts and bad choices experienced. It's easy to look at the outside of a person and make judgments. Stepping out of my comfort zone caused anxiety and made me wonder when I should speak to both of these ladies. In the past there were times when I was chastised for speaking out to those in power. Because of these ladies, I was gaining selfconfidence to stand up for the less fortunate. Always remember that the outside features of people can be deceiving. Look into their eyes and their hearts to find hurting hearts. Smiles don't always represent what is really happening in a person's private life.

My dearest diary, come, listen and walk on this dusty path of silence, and let's deal with the emotional experiences through words on my computer. I know you will not criticize or judge me. Here is my story.

Chapter 2

Good Homes Located

During the summer of 2005, I was looking for a good book for my English as a Second Language / English Language Learners conversation group, for whom I was the facilitator. The book needed to be filled with simple information on activities understandable for English Language Learners (ELL), people who were learning English as a Second Language (ESL). These were educational classes offered to all cultures studying beginning English.

One evening at a restaurant, a friend overheard me looking for an entertainment book with routes off the beaten fishing paths to explore and visit new places. My friend came over to our table and suggested an author. Timidly, I asked for more information.

The next night we met at a neighboring club. He brought me the author's book. It was filled with many basic vocabulary words that were used in simple sentences. I quickly glanced through the Texas book and noticed various pictures showing how and where to locate good fishing holes and places to experience nature's habitats. This book was perfect for my students. Locating something new for the students to learn from was pleasing.

That evening I viewed each page of the book. It was simple, informational—the group could even play games with the map of Texas. What a wonderful, relaxing way for the students to expand their vocabulary and reading skills and gain knowledge about a fabulous state. It would encourage the students to travel, take pictures, and return to class to share their experiences. I became super excited. As I looked at the last page, there was the author's phone number. The book was more than thirty years old. Would the author still have the same phone number?

My mind raced just to think about the big state of Texas. It has so many lakes and rivers, mostly man-made rivers, but there were excellent fishing places like Toledo Bend Lake and more than 1,200 miles of shoreline and thousands of wonderful streams. What a fabulous Texas book full of information and exciting areas to explore.

I wondered if the author was alive. Did she still have some extra books? Her fishing books would surely help my students see the value in learning English. They could travel with family and friends to the various locations they chose. What a great way to build and expand happy family relations.

That next afternoon I dashed home after work. Reaching for the phone, I suddenly stopped and looked at the phone number. Why should I be nervous? Perhaps it would be better for me to phone tomorrow. Why was I waiting? This book was a wonderful exploration book. What a great purpose, and so many fabulous lessons.

Smiling, I told myself that the author was simply a human being who wrote books and magazine articles to help inform readers about a subject. She understood about fishing and places to explore with family and friends.

I took a giant leap and boldly dialed that thirty-year-old phone number. Not realizing who answered the phone, I immediately started to explain how I was a volunteer facilitator for an English as a Second Language / English Language Learners conversation class at a nearby college. I was inquiring if the author had any of her Texas fishing books left to purchase for my students.

"Anita, someone is asking for you and wants to buy some of your Texas fishing books," said a voice on the other end of the line. The author must have been close to the phone because I could hear a woman's gentle voice in the background. She took the phone and said, "Hello." I carefully repeated myself, explaining my purpose for the call. She immediately asked, "Can you come over now?" Surprised, I was not ready for her quick response.

Of course, it would be my pleasure to drive over and meet this author. Then I could speak further about purchasing her books. The author tried to give me directions, but she eventually passed the phone on to the person who originally answered the phone. I said I would be over in about a half hour.

I was so excited. My heart jumped high with joy. What was so special about meeting this person? I remembered many years earlier working at a radio station, where I met Captain Waves, the biggest star in Hollywood. Yet he did nothing to make my heart jump for joy. Why was this woman, this author, activating my heart and emotions?

The beautiful blue sky and quiet afternoon breeze seemed to create positive conditions for us to meet. My mind traveled a mile a minute. First, I needed to get some gas for my car. Next, I dashed to the college to pick up our conversation group brochure. It would help verify the program I was talking about and the needs of the students for something easy to read.

The next step was to locate some flowers. I stopped at three different stores to look for some fresh and beautiful flowers, but nothing caught my eye. Then I noticed another local grocery store that had a fabulous florist department. Immediately, my eyes zoomed in on an astonishing arrangement of pink lilies and roses. The flowers' aroma surrounded my presence. While walking to the cashier, customers glanced at the flowers and commented on how beautiful the arrangement looked and how sweet the aroma was. There were nine pink lilies with greenery. In the middle of the lilies were three red roses.

The flowers' aroma filled my car. I was so proud of myself that I didn't pick out any kind of flowers. The choice was perfect. Suddenly, I realized it had been more than thirty minutes since I had said I would be over in about a half hour. I worried about making a bad impression but hoped the flowers would show appreciation and gratitude for her time and inviting me to her home. Perhaps she would realize how much her time was valued as she looked later at the beautiful flowers.

It surprised me that the directions to this author's home were easy to follow. There was a car parked near the family's driveway, and the driver was watching as I located the right address.

The author's driveway was double in size. It could easily park six cars. The next eye-opener came when I looked up toward a simple brick home with two huge bay windows out front. The atmosphere told me this was a home, not just a house. There was something about it that rocked my senses. It was a beautiful one-story brick home with a basement. The yard was well kept. I really felt at home as I stepped onto the driveway.

As I picked up the beautiful flowers from the back seat, my eyes glanced up at the first bay window above the driveway. I could see a dining room table where someone sat. Then my attention was drawn to the other bay window. My heart became so excited that I could hardly contain my emotions. Why? Was my heart so excited because I was going to meet an author in her private home and request some books? Meeting other authors had not produced heartfelt excitement. I was used to meeting people from all walks of life, yet my emotions were running wild.

I noticed a man looking out at me from the other bay window. He was motioning with his hand to someone across the other side of the room. I viewed an elderly woman with white glistening hair slowly crossing the room, passing the man who was still watching me. By the time I reached the top of the steps, this person had the front door wide open. She extended her papery thin hand out to greet me as she stated that her name was Anita. I introduced myself and thanked her for allowing me to come to her home. As we shook hands, my heart beat so wildly that I thought it was going to jump out of my chest. She said, "My pleasure to meet you too." Instead of letting go of my hand, she caressed it. In the depths of my heart, I knew I was welcomed.

As she held my hand, our eyes met. I realized she was checking out my inner soul. Her firm yet lightly shaking and frail hand kept holding on to mine. It seemed like minutes, but just a few seconds passed as we looked deeply into each other's eyes. Only we were not just looking into each other's eyes. She was looking directly into the deepest part of my soul. For several moments she dissected every room of my heart, soul, mind, my whole being. Our eyes kept meeting without a blink. What a humbling experience. She held her shoulders back and head high, which was something I had not seen in many people, including me.

More emotions erupted with this inquisitive handshake. Joy flooded my being, and I felt such honor to be in her presence. What a surprise it was to feel my heart pounding. The smiles on our faces made me feel like we had known each other all of our lives.

My senses expanded to a whole new level of understanding. This woman writer never demanded anything from me. I was looking face-to-face at a very frail, elderly lady who held her head up. I had expected a fifty-year-old woman to greet me. I had forgotten about time. It had been thirty-plus years since this author had written her book.

The author motioned with her hands for me to come inside her home. I handed her the flowers and informed this new acquaintance how much her time was appreciated. I did not know anything about this author other than what was printed on the back of her book. It mentioned that her articles had been written in countless travel and fishing magazines. She had taught outdoor nature writing and had traveled the world over.

The author did not introduce me to her caregiver, but she did direct me toward an elderly man sitting in a chair. "This is my husband, Tom. Isn't he cute?"

He responded with a congenial smile and said, "It's a pleasure to meet you."

And I replied, "My pleasure to meet you too."

Tom noticed the flowers. "How beautiful!" he delightedly commented. The author handed the flowers to the caregiver while Tom and I shook hands. Tom apologized for not being able to stand up because of weak legs. What gentle manners. What a gracious man. It crossed my mind that meeting these two people must be a very special providence from God Almighty. I had never before experienced this exciting peace in their presence.

The author stretched her hand out and motioned for me to sit down on the long sofa that was covered by a green blanket. I watched her gracefully glide over to her creamed-colored love seat. My eyes glanced up on the wall. It was filled with different types of swords. I did not ask about them because the mission for being in this home was to meet the author and see if some of her Texas fishing books were available to purchase.

Once again, this author looked directly into my eyes. Her look continued to penetrate into the depths of my whole being. For a moment I really thought I was in the presence of angels. My ears became extremely keen to her soft-spoken words but not the total environment.

I explained how I learned about her book. My heart wanted this author to realize how helpful her book would be for my students. It was a special educational book to me. Each student could expand their word banks and learn information from sentences while enjoying nature trips. She attentively listened to every word I said. What a very lovely smile and soft voice she had. This author asked me questions about the college. She wanted to know about what buildings were being built and how many students were presently attending. This was the opportunity to hand the author my class brochure in the hope of establishing trust between us. She reached out and took the information. Then she glanced over it and placed the brochure near her glasses. I kind of chuckled to myself, wondering if the author could actually read it without her glasses.

Meanwhile, the caregiver was sitting at the dining room table talking on the phone about me. I could hear her say that a *stranger* was in the family home, speaking about purchasing some books.

That person on the other end of the line must have approved for the caregiver to allow the author to give me some books. The author then instructed the caregiver to bring me fifteen of her books. As the caregiver was walking away, the author gave a stern look. When the caregiver returned, the author instructed her to hand the books to me. Our eyes kept meeting as the caregiver obeyed her client. What a wonderful, caring caregiver who wanted to protect her client. She was very alert to her responsibilities in contacting a family's relatives and informing them to my presence.

Then the caregiver returned to the dining room table and moved the flowers into the living room. The vase was placed on a beautiful hand-carved table between the author and her husband.

Passing me, the caregiver made a point to inform me that if I needed more books, the author's daughter would need to be notified again. Immediately, this author gave a very displeased look. It appeared she preferred to be in control. There was a keen awareness coming from Tom as he watched and strained to listen to our verbal exchange. Periodically, we smiled at each other. There was a twinkle in his eyes whenever the author's and his eyes met.

I stood up and presented some money to the author. It was more than a hundred dollars to cover the books and tax. The author motioned for me to put the money away. I told her that she had taken the time to write the book and that I felt she deserved to be paid for her time. This author glanced at her books. Her look penetrated my heart. Smiling, this gracious author said, "No money for my books from you. Let me know if you need more for your students." I told her again that it was her right to receive payment for her diligent work.

Once again this author's look informed me not to question her. In exchange for money, she gave me explicit instructions, "Locate good homes and never charge for my book." She had a commanding voice of authority.

There was something very special between this author and me because it was hard to say goodbye. This author spoke slowly but in complete sentences. Leaving, I thanked Tom for allowing me in their home as I shook his quivering hand. The author walked me to their front living room door. Time had flown by. I had visited with this inspirational author for an hour. The whole room had become filled with the fragrance of lilies and roses.

JJ Janice

It seemed like there were musical notes floating throughout the whole room. The positive energy followed us right to the front door. The flower's fragrance continued to dance as we said our goodbyes. Thinking back, my heart was so exuberant. I had hoped that the precious words "Thank you" were said to this author, but the sweet smell of flowers spoke louder than any verbal words.

The sweet smell of warmth and love continued to fill my whole being. About a half mile away from the author's home, I had to pull off to the side of the road. My emotions got the best of me. How I wept! This was a totally new experience. I felt like we had known each other forever, but why? Had we met before? I would need to search my memories. I kept feeling this special lady's gentle yet firm handshake. I looked at my hand, which still recalled the welcomed handshake.

I had never been stripped down to the depths of my heart before. My heart felt like it had been stripped of all negative issues and exposed to all goodness. It had been years since I had cried. But this wasn't crying. It was weeping. Happiness was overflowing in my heart, and my extremely happy smile just wasn't going away. Why did she refuse my money? I would keep my word to make sure her books received good homes. I just sat in my car and wept. What was happening to me? How dare anyone break into my safety box!

Finally, I started the car to continue the drive home. Passing the community college, I could tell that our soccer team must have won their game because horns were blowing. I, too, had had a winning day.

Chapter 3

The Book Comes Alive

The conversation group was a free English class for beginner students to expand their English language. The class presented the opportunity for students to expand their English vocabulary, apply reading skills, and practice general English conversations on field trips. Doors of adventures and opportunities were wide open to students. The class offered speaking opportunities while studying fishing and exploring Texas. What a great confidence builder.

The fishing book was perfect for our class because it constantly challenged them to read and understand simple sentences with short paragraphs. Sometimes pictures inspired and encouraged a weekend trip with loved ones. They'd keep those memories for years to come.

The results were very positive. Over the next two weeks, several students drove out and personally experienced a multitude of fishing holes identified in the book. Each student's travel presentation supported other students and passionately encouraged them to expand their travels and then share experiences.

What a fabulous way to learn English without a bunch of stress. Students gained confidence through exploration. Their presentations encouraged closer attention and listening skills by including maps, pictures, and brochures. They encouraged one another to travel and learn to fish. Each student advanced in asking questions, and their desire to communicate with other cultures grew. Students from various countries realized they had many things in common, especially families exploring together. The students enjoyed playing games with maps and learning to ask questions. *How far away is the river? How long does it take to drive there? Was a tent needed to stay overnight? Was the river to the east, west, north, or south of the college?* These questions advanced to higher thinking skills. Students needed to use both the brain's input to come up with questions and the output to ask them. What fun the students had exploring how to speak the English language.

During the third week of class, I contacted the author again, requesting additional books for my other English class. Speaking with the author over the phone, I could tell she was exuberantly happy to hear from me. She immediately asked me to come visit her. My heart was thrilled. I could not stop smiling.

Thinking about meeting the author again engulfed my whole being. Just driving up to her driveway caused my heart to do flips. Looking up at the large bay window, I saw Tom waving to me. I waved back. We flashed big smiles at each other. The author gracefully walked across her living room to the front door, passing Tom sitting in his rocker.

Of course, this time I brought yellow carnation flowers without a vase. I always wanted to show them how honored I was that they were welcoming me back inside their home. My heart hoped their front door would be wide open.

By the time I reached the top of the steps, that front door was wide open. Instead of a handshake, two arms stretched out to greet me. As we embraced, my hands felt that she had very frail and thin shoulder blades.

On this occasion I met a different caregiver. I recognized that she was the person sitting in her car that first time I had driven up to the family's home. She must have deeply cared about this couple and wanted to make sure they were protected from me for whatever reason.

Tom and I shook hands. Then his eyes smiled when he became aware of the flowers. "Oh, beautiful!" Tom stated. Then the caregiver took the flowers, placed them in a light pink vase with water, and brought them back into the living room. Like the lilies, these flowers were set on the hand-carved European round table. They were less fragrant.

The caregiver turned and looked at me. She bent down as she passed by and said, "My name is Winnie."

I quietly told her, "JJ." We smiled and she gave a quick wink.

Excited, the author asked me how the students responded to her fishing book. While we were talking, I heard Winnie on the phone. She was telling the author's daughter that the *stranger* was in her parent's home again. Winnie must have told her that the stranger wanted more books. The caregiver alerted the author that her daughter had granted permission for the additional books.

The author's eyes spoke stronger than her words. She motioned to the caregiver to bring twenty more books. I perceived that this author expected to have full authority in making her own decisions.

The author surprised me by saying, "I am sorry that I can no longer sign my name. My hands do not work very well. I will not be able to sign each book." I dismissed the offer right away. I had not expected such action, but it was sweet of her nonetheless.

We talked about her book's success among the students. The author's face beamed. Her eyes sparked. Her smile showed happiness. This impressed me, knowing she was pleased with the reading and activities results. I could tell this author's heart felt very pleased to know what she had written years earlier was still useful.

As I gazed upon the author's face, I noticed that she was happy that she was helping educate students. Then my attention suddenly centered on her face. There were no wrinkles. She was still an attractive woman. It was interesting how I had not observed this during our previous meeting.

My mind returned to our conversation, and together, we understood the value of knowledge through new books. This was vital to each student's confidence in learning a new language.

Meanwhile in the living room corner, Tom was listening closely to our conversation. He was straining to hear what we were saying. Sometimes he would say, "What! What!" Then the author would tell her husband to turn up his hearing aid, and she explained our conversation. What a very precious couple. I also noticed that there were sparks of love between them as they spoke together. It was evident in their eyes that there was a deep communication of respect between this husband and wife. How refreshing.

This time I didn't offer the author any money for her books. I informed her that each previous book for the conversation group class had a *good home* and that each had been well received. As I was leaving the author's living room, Tom's voice strained to speak, "Nice to have seen you again." His trembling, weak voice still remains in my heart. I shook his bony hand and said, "It has been my pleasure to have seen you again too."

The author slowly walked me to their front door. She repeated that I should just let her know if I needed more books. I glanced at Winnie, and we smiled at each other. I asked the author if she would like to hear how the second group of students responded to her book. The author said, "Come back." We gave each other a light hug, and I informed her I would report back how the second class of students enjoyed her book. What a delightful lady to be around. It was a relief to know our paths would cross again.

A couple of weeks later, I phoned the author to report how the second class liked her book. She asked me to come over. Delighted, I immediately accepted the invitation. We spoke about the book's success and how some of the students visited various places.

During this visit I blurted out to the author, "How would you like to be our guest author?" Her eyes popped wide open. I hadn't planned on saying this. I just blurted it out. I shocked myself! Winnie was always listening very closely to our conversations. Immediately in a very low voice, she sternly informed me that the author could not make this decision.

It hadn't occurred to me that I might need someone's permission for this author to come to my class. Yes, she was elderly, but she could certainly think and speak for herself. What had I missed? I thought about my own mother, who was ninety-six. We helped her walk now, but she still made her own decisions.

The author inquired, "How would I get to your class?" I mentioned that I could pick her up and drive her to the event. She was so elated that she immediately asked, "Where is your car?"

I replied with a little chuckle, "It's in your driveway."

Winnie and I were totally caught off guard when the author instantly rose from the cream-colored love seat and motioned for me to follow her. The author showed me the back stairs and led me down the back way through the basement to the downstairs back door onto the driveway. Winnie rushed to keep up with us. We were both concerned about how fast this elderly woman could move. Then she went straight to my old car, opened the passenger side door, climbed right onto the seat, and said, "See, I can do it!"

Scoreboard

Author: 1; Alzheimer's: 0

My dearest diary, this author did not even hesitate to climb onto the front seat when she saw my car. She just opened up that passenger door and climbed right in. My eyes watched this frail, limber body climb into a sitting position on the front seat. What determination! The author looked so comfortable and proud, filled with accomplishment. She quietly repeated, "I can do it." What confidence and peacefulness her voice projected as she proudly presented her smile of accomplishment to the caregiver and me.

I glanced up and noticed Tom intensely watching all of us from the bay window. His body strained forward, and his face was solemn as he observed our actions with his wife in the driveway. There was no smile or waving. He watched us as far as he could view us until we walked out of his sight back to the basement.

I assured Winnie that I would make sure this gifted writer stayed safe. The author heard us and informed Winnie, "She can pick me up."

At the top of the stairs, Winnie took my arm. The author continued to walk away from us, returning to her love seat. Winnie informed me that this special lady had Alzheimer's disease. I was stunned. What did that even mean? What was she even talking about? My knowledge was very limited, and I really did not understand much about this subject.

Winnie told me that we would need to contact Lynn, the author's daughter. Plus the service agency would need to give their okay too. I asked Winnie if Lynn was in charge of her parents. Winnie nodded and cautioned me that this very special author might not even remember I had visited or asked her to be the guest author.

I had a minor experience several years earlier with Alzheimer's when a friend's wife had a devastating memory claimer. She had become aware of women talking with her husband. My friend asked me to take his wife out of the room during one of our meetings because she was starting to become nervous. I had known her for years, and she recognized and trusted me, so we started walking to a different area. I remembered looking at her face when I started to close the other room's door. Her eyes became wide, and she started turning her head, looking around for her husband. I became a little scared because he was not with us. I was not sure what to do or how to handle her, so I started to tell her that her husband was coming shortly. She looked toward the shut door and luckily saw him come out to join us. He was a welcoming sight for both of us.

As for this author, I did not even pick up on any signs that would indicate she had Alzheimer's. There were no signs that her memory was leaving as we spoke about students and her book. The writer spoke a little slower and could not sign her name any longer, but it just did not dawn on me that her mind was fading away and how far along she was in this dark illness.

Once again, Winnie contacted Lynn. The protective daughter would meet with various people and have an open discussion. Together, Lynn, the caregivers, and the agency would need to agree on what was best for the author. Was she able to go out in public? I just could not understand all the commotion.

One of my coworkers' father had Alzheimer's. He was forgetful, but the family constantly took him out to restaurants and family activities like attending birthday parties and going to the beach. They ordered food for him when he forgot what he wanted, but they included him as much as possible. The same was true of my other friend until his wife started to sometimes shout in public. Perhaps the author was at this stage.

My lack of knowledge showed my naivete regarding the steps of Alzheimer's. A six-week period before the day of the guest author's arrival at class would give everyone ample time to make some decisions. Her caregivers and family would decide who would drive this author. They needed to figure out if the author was capable of handling a public appearance.

The caregivers' agency wanted to meet and speak directly with me. They asked me detailed questions "How long does the class meet? How many students are in the class? What does the room look like, and what's the size? Who will be asking questions? What do you know about Alzheimer's disease? Do you have Lynn's phone number and email?"

Lynn gave strict instructions to the agency that no one was to ask any questions of her mother, not the students or me. We all still had time to decide who would drive the author to the class.

The author *remembered* that I had asked her to come to our class. That special morning Winnie helped the author with her makeup, chose proper clothes, and prepared Anita's hair for her special day. Lynn drove her to the college.

Scoreboard

Author: 2; Alzheimer's: 0

This author was an author, and that's the way my mind referred to her. I couldn't relate to her by her first name. There wasn't any personal connection. Perhaps over time I would call her by her name, Anita.

Chapter 4

Guest Author Day

On July 18, the conversation group ordered a special cake and flowers for the Guest Author Day. I had given each student a little information about our guest author and Alzheimer's disease. I explained to the group that we were not allowed to ask the author any questions because she might get embarrassed if she didn't know how to give an answer. The students were so understanding and caring. I admired each one of them.

I also explained to the class that this special author had received more than fifteen awards as an outdoor writer. She wrote for fishing magazines and taught for many years, helping students and the public explore local nature field trips. It was a time of mixed joys and sorrows, realizing her age and illness with Alzheimer's.

In the previous class, we had spoken about parents and the stress of watching them grow old and how it affected our own experiences. Listening as the students spoke about their different cultures and how they dealt with aging was a great eye-opener. We discussed firsthand how the inner design of families from around the world handled aging. The time was informative and impressive.

That special day, Lynn parked far away from the building where the class was meeting. The author and Lynn slowly walked across campus, looking at the various buildings and seeing hundreds of students dashing to their classes. The college's president was taking his normal afternoon walk around campus. Being an alert and caring gentleman, he introduced himself to them. They spoke for a while. Then he directed them to the right building. I don't know if Lynn mentioned her mother's purpose at the college. Perhaps he did not know the impact this author had made on so many students' lives as an instructor for more than twenty-five years at this college.

Mother and daughter arrived by the east door of the visitor's building. Meanwhile, I was waiting by the south door. One of the students ran outside and informed me that the author and her daughter had arrived. Walking toward the classroom, my eyes spotted a tall, slender woman with short, dark brown hair. I sized her up as the author's daughter. My eyes also noticed the author sitting with the students inside the classroom. I had missed the great opportunity to greet both of them, but the students never missed a beat. They welcomed the guests and asked the author to come join them in the conversation room.

Lynn watched my every step as I approached her. She was not smiling. She had beady eyes that made me feel like laughing. Immediately, I sensed Lynn's devotion to her mother. Lynn firmly instructed, "Remember, there will be no questions asked of my mother." There was a total difference between Lynn's tones compared to that of her mother. The author's voice was commanding and represented respect, but the daughter's voice was demanding.

While we firmly shook hands, Lynn added, "My mother is sitting down in the classroom. What do you think about people who have been in jail?"

Where did this come from? What triggered that comment? I thought fast and stated, "It doesn't matter." Lynn gave an okay look. Together, we entered the small classroom, and I greeted the author, "Welcome to our Guest Author Day. It is very good to have you come and be part of our class."

The author appeared totally delighted to be present. She gazed upon each student as they spoke their names and countries of origin. Meanwhile, Lynn observed the entire class and did not say a word. No smiles came from her eyes, and her lips didn't crack in a grin. Yet I viewed this very slender woman with compassion. Those beady eyes showed concern for her mother. There was a deep protective love for this elderly author who penetrated the whole room.

That special day our conversation group brought happiness to this author. What a pleasure it was for the students. Not everything went perfect that special day. I could see in the students' eyes that they wanted to ask questions just like me and to talk with the author, but we all honored Lynn's directions by not posing any questions. Each student was invited to speak with the guest author and tell her what her book meant to him or her.

Sadly, there were a few students who felt English was a language barrier. Did they feel that their speaking skills were not advanced enough, or was this the case because we were instructed not to ask questions? What question would they have asked if they could have? Perhaps they wondered if the author had traveled to their country. We took two individual pictures with the author—one for the author and one for the student to remember this day. Their individual smiles reflected the joy in meeting this author in person.

Lynn listened closely to how her mother's book helped different students advance in their English skills. Her eyes scanned the environment, and her acute ears were wide open, listening to each student speak as she made sure everyone minded their p's and q's. Perhaps Lynn wanted to see if the students (or me) would sneak in a question or two. Truth be told, without the questions, the event was a bit boring.

I noticed that Lynn was starting to thaw a little. While we were taking pictures together, a little smile crept on Lynn's face. Next, we watched a very short film about the state of Texas. The guest author appeared to enjoy the short travel film; however, even only seven minutes in duration, it was too long. It would have been nice if the students could have asked Lynn, Anita's daughter, some questions. However, perhaps that might upset Lynn's mom.

The group appeared to savor these moments together. What a wonderful class. Then suddenly, Lynn and I noticed the author had a somewhat frightened look in her eyes.

Scoreboard

Author: 2; Alzheimer's: 1

I think the students noticed this too. I asked Lynn if her mother would like some cake. The cake had the Spanish greeting *Bienvenido, Gracias*. I was told it meant, "Welcome, Thank You." Lynn looked directly into her mother's eyes and slowly spoke, "Mom, would you like a piece of cake?" Instantly, this brought the author back to our reality.

Scoreboard

Author: 3; Alzheimer's: 1

Quickly, I asked the students to help set up the table and bring the cake over for a picture. A very special moment came when I saw the author lift her eyes and make sure every student had a piece of cake before she began eating too. What a wonderful caring heart. Before I took another group picture, I noticed a little piece of frosting on the left side of the author's mouth. I gently wiped the frosting off, and I caught Lynn noticing this action in my peripheral vision. Her icy eyes melted some more.

Perhaps the realization of Alzheimer's started to set in as some of the students stepped away from the table after they ate some of the delicious Mexican tres leches cake and started to point to the world map, talking about their home countries. Others helped clean up the table. Everyone was so respectful. It was a great eye-opener to Alzheimer's harsh realities, especially for me. I entertained the thought that perhaps this outing was too much for this author.

Thanks to the cake, the class was able to continue with conversations. The students kept their voices low in an effort not to overstimulate the author. They were so understanding and compassionate. These precious moments filled my heart with joy. How I admired each of them.

JJ Janice

Time flew by so fast. Suddenly, I became aware that the class was nearing its close. Lynn and I could tell it was time to return the author to the comfort of her private love seat. As the conversation group was concluding, I requested each student thank the author by giving their names again and speaking in their native language. Each said, "Thank you for coming today."

When a student said he was from Mexico, the author responded in Spanish. Another student from the Ukraine spoke in Russian, and it turned out that the author knew Russian, so they had a short conversation. The same happened when students spoke in Portuguese, French, Chinese, German, and Japanese. What a wonderful lesson it had become. Each student was a cherry on top of a hot fudge sundae.

After class Lynn informed me that her dad knew even more languages than her mother. Wow! What kind of quality adventures this family must have had, learning about cultures around the world and foreign languages firsthand.

Lynn asked me to stay and watch her mother while she brought the car to the south door. I felt humbled and privileged she trusted me with this responsibility.

By this time all of the students had departed for their next class. For a few minutes, it was just the author and me walking slowly arm in arm down the short hallway toward the south door. As we locked arms, I held the author's left hand. I softly spoke to her, thanking her for coming to our conversation group's class. I hoped she enjoyed being on campus and being with the students. She clamped onto my hand with hers. Once again, we looked into each other's eyes, and I knew then that I would always remember that familiar smile.

Before walking outside, my author leaned her head on my shoulder. Such warmth encompassed my heart. Lynn had not arrived with the car. It was a relief because I was not sure how she would have responded. She might have become very upset. After all, she was her mother's protector.

After driving up to the south entrance, Lynn opened the passenger's door. I helped our author in the front passenger's seat and buckled her up for safety. I whispered, "Thank you for coming.

I love you," and I gave her a quick kiss on her right cheek. A huge smile came from my author, but she never looked at me. I noticed that Lynn had placed the flower gifts in the back seat. As she opened the driver's side door and climbed into the car, we smiled at each other.

One last time I thanked Lynn for allowing her mother to attend our conversation class. I hoped the time had not exhausted her mother too much. I commented about how the cake and the many different languages had saved the class lesson.

Both of us shared a very hardy laugh as we waved to each other and departed in different directions. What a fabulous day. It was a day filled with memories for so many people. How long would our guest author remember this special day?

My dearest diary, that afternoon turned out to be extremely special to our students, Lynn, the author, and me. I realized that this special author must have felt a sense of closure. She was able to walk one last time on her beloved campus where she had taught for so many years.

By the next week's class, we had developed the pictures from the event. Each student wrote something simple to our guest author on a three-by-five-inch card. Together, we created a special memory album. The student's note cards were meant simply to *thank* the guest author. It was a writing lesson from each of the student's heart. The author knew nothing about this creative memory album.

The following month I took the memory album to the guest author. I knew it would be bad form to ask this author if a student or two could accompany me to her home. The students and I hoped by looking through the album, she would somehow remember that special meeting with so many students from around the world. We all greatly appreciated her time and enjoyed expanding our English skills through her book.

That day I closely observed her slowly thumb through the memory album, which the class had titled *A Visit with Our Guest Author*. As Anita glanced at each picture and what was written, it dawned on me that day must have been very special because the author's eyes sparkled. Our hearts were filled with great joy and peace, and I reported these precious moments back to the class. Our wish for her had come true. As an ESL instructor and facilitator, watching Anita's smile reminded me how vitally important she must have been to her past students. Lives had been filled with hope. Learning English was so crucial to communicating.

In the back of the memory album, I added pictures of a vacation to the Oregon Coast. The blue skies of Texas reminded me of the ocean. Perhaps the rolling waves would remind her of the rolling clouds that sometimes overpowered the Texas blue sky.

Scoreboard

Author: 4; Alzheimer's: 1

Chapter 5

Birthday Surprise

The flu and sinus infections had impacted my health, so I didn't contact Anita for several months. It surprised me how quickly time had passed, and not even a thought crossed my mind to contact my author even during the holidays. However, on a late day in March, the sun was very warm. Suddenly, she was constantly on my mind. From the time I woke up, Anita did not leave my thoughts. In the middle of that early sunny Saturday afternoon, I finally took the chance to contact this beautiful lady who lived a life far different than mine. Now I was really thinking about Anita and not calling her *author*.

Lynn answered the phone and instructed, "Come on over. It's my mom's birthday." My heart instantly became excited. When I knew that my family was okay and that the cleaning chores had been completed, I dashed over to the birthday store and bought what I thought was the best birthday card to brighten Anita's special day. It was on yellow paper, and it showed the sun shining through the trees and a mountain range in the background. When the card opened, the happy birthday song played. Inside was another picture of the sun shining over the mountain range, but it opened to a green meadow. The artist had made the picture look so relaxing.

I dashed to my favorite flower shop and explained the special occasion to the employee. She suggested roses with some greenery. I listened closely as the flower specialist explained the roses would last longer by changing the water and peeling off the outside petals as they began to shrivel and die. This action would extend the flowers' life. Hopefully, the flowers would continue to look fresh for a good week or more and radiate joy whenever Anita and Tom looked at them.

For one of our class potlucks, a Korean student brought a fabulous sweet potato cake. It did not have any processed sugar, but it tasted sweet. I didn't know if this elderly writer had any issues with her health like diabetes. She looked very healthy, but I didn't know for sure, so I dashed over to the Korean market. Luckily, the Korean bakery had one of these sweet potato cakes left on their shelf.

As I drove up the family's driveway, I saw Lynn mowing the small lawn. She immediately stopped working and rushed over to my car. Much time had passed since the day with the guest author, but it felt like no time had transpired when we saw each other's face. I barely stepped out of the car when two long, skinny arms extended toward me. "Wow!" said Lynn. "You really know how to hug." It's true. I do enjoy good, meaningful hugs from people. This was an exceptionally precious moment that called for an exceptionally wonderful hug.

Lynn looked deep into my eyes just like her mother. Of course, I did the same in return. Then we embraced again with laughter. That sound of laughter was so precious. It still lingers in my memory and brings a warm smile to my happy face.

I noticed that Lynn had a great tan. When I asked about it, Lynn told me I could go to the local grocery store and purchase fake suntan lotion. It was amazing what this suntan lotion could do during our gloomy December and light winter season. We looked at each other and immediately burst out with laughter again. She also pointed out that by coloring my silver hair, I would look at least ten years younger. I told her I had colored my hair before—even used a washout—but neither one had turned out very well. In fact, people didn't even recognize me. Then she inquired if I ever planned to get a tattoo. I looked at Lynn, and I had a great laugh.

Glancing up at the large bay window, I saw Tom wave to us. We waved back. Then he must have motioned to Anita that the two of us were talking together in the driveway. I could see Anita crossing the living room, strolling toward the front door. I came to understand how Lynn loved bringing surprises to her parents.

My dearest diary, Lynn could really be so funny sometimes. She liked taking care of her parents' yard because they paid for her services. "I like money," she commented. Then she instantly added how her back filled with pain whenever she did the yard work. She wasn't sure how much longer she would be able to help with the yard. She showed me her back brace.

I opened the back passenger-side car door and handed Lynn the sweet potato cake and camera. My hands carried the pink flower arrangement and card. Surprisingly, Lynn locked her right arm with my left arm, and together, we walked up the narrow steps to the front door. Well, actually, it was two grown women, one very slender and one very heavy, trying to walk arm in arm up the narrow steps where overgrown shrubs lined both sides.

Looking back, it amazed me that neither of us tripped over each other or even dropped the cake into the shrubs. Bet that would have made her father and mother laugh, seeing two grown women trying to catch a cake falling to the ground. In Peru and Korea and probably other countries too, closeness between people includes locking arms together while walking. This was another very precious time to remember.

Arriving at the family's front door, Anita greeted me with her arms stretched out for a hug. As we gently embraced, I felt Anita's shoulder blades. Lynn smiled and then excused herself to put away the gardening tools, taking the cake and camera with her.

As Anita and I were walking inside the entryway, the caregiver took the flowers. I kept the card. Then came another surprise. Anita took my arm in her arm, and together, we slowly strolled into the living room. Tom and I gave a short hug as we greeted one another. "Pleased to see you again."

Our eyes locked, and I graciously responded, "Very nice to see you again too."

Anita sat on her love seat, and I sat on the green couch. She turned to Tom and requested that he turn down his loud symphony music. (He was extremely deaf.) Being a gentleman of manners, he turned down the music and apologized that it had been so loud.

Winnie placed the flower arrangement and vase on the homemade carved table that separated Anita and Tom. I wondered what was taking Lynn so long. It crossed my mind that maybe she was curious about the pictures on my camera. There were pictures of many students showing off their presentation skills, including those reading her mother's book. The individuals presented places where they had traveled. I hoped Lynn was looking through the pictures and possibly observing how her mother's books were utilized for educational purposes.

Suddenly, I questioned myself, *Why am I here?* I was so excited and honored to see these three people again and celebrate Anita's birthday with them in such a very simple way. All of us kept smiling, holding conversations about the weather, students, school activities, even what the spring season would bring along with fresh new flowers and green leaves on the trees. People would take vacations and cook homemade foods at family barbeques. Everyone would want to talk about their adventures. All of the people together would fill the atmosphere with *joy*. I no longer questioned being invited to this special day's celebration.

About fifteen minutes later, Lynn joined us. She looked like she had opened the cookie jar and had gotten caught eating the last freshly baked cookie. She handed me the camera without looking at my face. I handed her the birthday card and looked at her face. Lynn walked over and sat next to her mom.

The card was not sealed, so Anita could easily open it with her fingers. Her small-motor skills still worked to some degree. The card's font was smaller than I had realized. Anita strained to read the words. Lynn gently took her finger and pointed to each word as she slowly read the sentences to her mother. How delightful to see a daughter point to words as she read. I could picture Anita doing the same with Lynn when Lynn was a small child. She explained that it was a birthday card. When Anita opened the card, her eyes sparkled as she listened to the music. I wondered how long it would be before Anita would forget about this special day. I wondered if it would be her last birthday.

Scoreboard

Anita: 4; Alzheimer's: 2

Lynn must have been thinking the same thoughts. Suddenly, she looked at me and asked a random question. She wanted to know if I could do push-ups? What a wonderful way to take a sad moment and turn it into something funny. I replied, "No, I am too fat. If I lose a good thirty pounds, maybe I could, but I doubt it. Why? Can you?" Lynn immediately took the challenge and dropped to the floor and started to do three push-ups. Then she stood up, looked at me, and pulled an inhaler apparatus out from her front pocket. I glanced at her parents, and they were just staring at Lynn. It was really hard for me not to burst out laughing when I saw that inhaler hanging halfway out of her mouth and this very thin, well-kept woman still huffing and puffing. Lynn smiled and then commented, "I need a smoke."

It was very interesting to observe how a person's mind works. Something about the push-ups triggered Anita to speak about Lynn trying out for the swim and high-dive teams years earlier at the nearby high school. Lynn gave her mother a very displeased look. Lynn explained how just before diving off the high dive, she noticed her mother watching and instantly lost her concentration. She didn't enter the water smoothly like a whale's tail. Disappointed, Lynn neither made the high-dive team nor the swim team. It must have been one of those seasonal moments in time that both mother and daughter never forgot. Later Lynn brought up that she had never forgiven her mother or herself for that failure.

Meanwhile, during this birthday visit, we discussed working and earning money. Lynn worked at a gym. It was her responsibility to have the gym's front door open by five in the morning. She liked knowing the owners relied and trusted her with the company's keys. I wondered why this was so important to her, but I never asked.

JJ Janice

We four talked about the flowers and plants in the family's yard. I asked why the shrubs were not cut down lower so that Anita and Tom had a better view of Chess Bay. They told me that by trimming the shrubs lower, the neighbor's noise came into the family's yard. Sometimes the noise was so loud that it seeped through the shrubs. Lynn explained that her parents loved having outdoor patio parties during the summer, and the shrubs provided privacy.

The conversations continued with more smiles and laughter. Suddenly, Lynn and her father joined together to sing a family remembrance song that even included a train whistle sound. This brought another wonderful smile to Anita's face. This family enjoyed being together.

Time passed so quickly. We shared three hours of great conversation and laughter. Lynn needed to do the weekly grocery shopping for her parents. She asked me to remain with her parents until she returned. Winnie strongly stated, "No! You both need to leave." Well, we knew who was in charge. I found out later staying so long often meant Anita would likely be hard to handle the next day because of the previous day's stimulation. Winnie asked me to please only stay twenty minutes if I returned to visit Anita.

We all hugged goodbye. Then Lynn and I walked arm in arm out the front door and down the steps to our cars without falling into the shrubbery. I was about to enter my car when I glanced up at the big bay window and noticed Tom waving to us. Together, Lynn and I gave a hearty smile and waved back. What a delightful afternoon.

Driving home, the leftover fragrance of roses danced around in my mind. The memory brought a peaceful smile to my mind. I was very pleased this common stranger had accepted their very special invitation to their private birthday celebration. Again, my mind wondered if Anita would live another year.

Chapter 6

The Good Life

Several months later on a very hot summer Saturday, we visited together again. Once again, I purchased flowers. This time chrysanthemums would enhance their living room. I turned off the car's engine and wiped the sweat off my face. I really thought I could handle the heat walking from my car to their front door. Tom was not in his recliner, waving to me, but I could see Anita scooting across the living room, traveling fast toward the front door.

As I arrived at the front door, I saw that Anita's arms were not stretched out. She looked sternly at my face. Gently, she lifted her boney right hand and wiped the moisture from my brow with her nimble fingers. I noticed she left the dampness on her fingers. I apologized for the wetness. How embarrassing!

Then it happened. My heart started beating so fast. I was overwhelmed with joy as Anita stretched her very thin arms out to greet me. "I have been waiting for you," she whispered in my ear as we embraced. Her body felt so brittle. I wondered if her other bones felt the same way. It seemed like we held on to each other for eternity. Her arms encompassed my shoulders. The hold was firm, and it felt like the pressure went all the way to my insides. I almost started to cry, feeling her love for me. Hearing Anita speak those precious words was so special. I wanted to tell her I missed her too.

After sitting down, we briefly spoke about the students' learning. Anita was trying to explain the importance of understanding different cultures and customs from her travel experiences. And we compared that to my simply reading books and meeting people from different cultures in class. I experienced how Anita must have spoken with her students, electrifying their ears so they would listen closely and learn how to better identify the needs of all cultures.

I mentioned that my only out-of-the-country experience was the wonderful people, cultures, lands, and food of Peru, especially Lima and Chimbota. Her eyes lit up, and she commented that if we had met ten years earlier, we could have written a book together about our experiences in South America. I mentioned how that would have been exciting. We could have even traveled to see how our visiting countries had expanded their economies. She flashed that smile of acceptance. Unfortunately, no one can turn back time.

The best way to travel and explore new places was always in person. It helped people appreciate where they lived and witness the living conditions of various cultures. Anita mentioned, "When traveling, you can expand cultural awareness just by walking down various city side streets, going through museums, sitting on a bench near a shopping center, or relaxing and having coffee or tea in a cafe while glancing at the various people." She mentioned that a good doughnut shop was always restful. Some countries served cheese and wine instead of a full meal either in the afternoon or at nighttime. Life was exciting and wonderfully memorable. Anita commented, "Looking back, I've lived a good life."

The subject became even more personal when I mentioned my stomach did not like spicy foods, except some light spicy foods or rice dishes from Mexico, India, and Bangladesh. My background was German. My mother cooked blander foods, especially goulash. She made tasty home-cooked chicken (with lard), potato salad, and pies.

Then Anita changed the subject to the best way to produce wine and what foods matched up with different wines. I told her about how my mother picked very tasty vegetables from the garden but that we only had one apple tree. I would climb that tree, sit on a firm branch, and enjoy eating freshly picked apples. Talking with Anita during this time, I would never have known she had Alzheimer's.

Anita alerted me, "Growing our own vegetable gardens was healthier for our bodies." I totally agreed. We wondered how many people planted and grew their own vegetable gardens and through their diligent work provided many good meals.

Scoreboard

Anita: 5; Alzheimer's: 2

I briefly mentioned that my mother would speak German at church but would not teach us German. Anita spoke something in German. I said all I knew was how to say, "Good morning," and, "Good night." She gave me a baffled look. Her Alzheimer's could not stop us from coming up with simple conversations while reminiscing about some of our experiences.

As I was standing up about to leave, I alerted Anita that my hubby and I would be vacationing in South Dakota for the next couple of weeks. Anita looked into my eyes and said, "Think about old Anita. I will remember you every day." My mind jolted. This was an instant verbal shock to my ears, and I fought back my tears. I did not view her as old. There is a difference between being old and being feeble.

I glanced to my left and noticed the end table had a miniature manger scene, but Jesus was not in the manger. All the other parts were together. I realized Anita must be a Christian and possibly a prayer warrior. But Lynn had said her mother was an atheist. Atheists didn't keep nativity scenes in their homes.

During the next visit after I returned from vacation, a conversation stuck out in my memory, one pertaining to a disagreement Anita had with her hubby. Tom wanted to move to Asia because he loved the people and culture. Anita begged him to remain with the family. Anita quietly mentioned she seldom begged. Once, she begged in front of a judge when Lynn was incarcerated for possession of marijuana in her young adult years, and the second time involved convincing Tom not to leave the family and live in another country.

Anita advised talking together as husband and wife was vitally important and respecting different views or opinions relieved some of their marital pressures. Differences of opinions sometimes produced conflicts and stresses. Then looking somewhat disgusted, she changed the subject. Anita just could not understand why Lynn married so often. Anita was very pleased that her last marriage had lasted, but she felt sorry for her hubby. Lynn mentioned when her mother and hubby first met, her mother handed him a "fix it" list of items for around their home. Lynn had informed her mother that her special man could fix anything. Then the subject changed again, and Anita informed me that Tom had suffered several heart attacks. I never exactly knew what subjects Anita wanted to explore with short conversations. I questioned if she was saying goodbye to these various subjects.

We agreed that divorce would always be the last straw; however, it is far better to be divorced than to be abused. It is better to be single and lonely than married and sorry. I mentioned that I had been married for forty-eight years and was looking forward to celebrating fifty. Anita looked very pleased.

Then the subject changed. She looked into my eyes and said, "I am glad to be alive. You are the icing on my cake." There is a huge difference between icing on the cake and frosting on a cake. I wished a family member or the caregiver had heard Anita say those words.

After several small conversations, I knew it was time to leave. Winnie didn't have to ask me. As I stood up, Anita rushed past me. I was scared she would fall down. She did not even use a cane. In fact, Lynn told me her mother would not use a cane because it was for "old people."

To my surprise, Anita brought out a nature picture. The picture was beautifully painted. It was a simple nature scene with animals. I looked at Anita, and then my mouth dropped open as I gazed upon the high quality of art. Anita smiled and stated, "This is for you. Remember me." She reached out for me to take the painting, but it remained in her hands. The caregiver came into the room and asked us about the picture. She stood beside Anita, looked at the beautiful art, and instructed me through her nod to take the painting. I hesitated, but the caregiver insisted that I accept the gift. Perhaps this was another goodbye to Anita's bucket list.

Next, Anita did an amazing thing. She held on to the painting and tried to peel off the green backing. Once again I told her that this painting really belonged to the family and perhaps some family member would like it. Well, that was incorrect according to her. Meanwhile, Winnie alerted Anita that the nature picture was glued onto the green backing. Anita looked again at the picture and then handed it to me.

My eyes gazed upon the quail hiding in the greenery with light pink flowers and the chipmunks looking up to the blue sky from their burrows. To this day, I still can't read the artist's name. Wish people would write their names clearer. What beautiful art though! Perhaps this picture was one less precious memory to check off on her memory bucket list. Anita must have sensed we both loved nature.

Scoreboard

Anita: 6; Alzheimer's: 3 (both won)

Then Anita bent down and handed me two smooth rocks. She had a dish filled with small rocks that had caught my eye on several visits. I really wanted to ask about those round rocks, but I felt like it wasn't any of my business. She mentioned that instead of purchasing candy when Tom and she traveled around the world, they would locate a river near the town and find a smooth rock. These rocks connected the world between cultures and countries. That rock collection represented a round world filled with adventure, caring hearts, and love. What a great way to remember cultures.

Oh, my dearest diary, I so do value these gifts. They have no monetary value. The value comes from a gift given from one heart to another.

Two weeks later I contacted Anita to see if it was a good day to visit. We shared the usual conversations, but this visit Anita looked out of the big bay window more than usual. Perhaps she was tired. We needed to cut visiting time short, so I requested permission to say Hello and Goodbye to Tom, who was sitting in the TV room.

Walking back into the living room, Anita's and my eyes joined. The caregiver was kneeling beside Anita. "Is she the one?" inquired the caregiver.

"Yes," Anita responded in a very weak voice.

Surprisingly, the caregiver asked me to stay for a few more minutes. I returned to the green couch and listened. Anita slowly explained the importance of her private book collections. Lynn had told her mother that all those books were either going into the garbage or would be burned. Anita asked if I would take all the books downstairs for safekeeping, and without any hesitation, I agreed. The books were downstairs on a large bookshelf that I had noticed months earlier. I needed to clean out a place for them. The caregiver told me it was important to pick up the books as soon as possible. Looking back, Anita must have noticed this area of her mind blacking out. Anita wanted control of her love for books. She didn't want Alzheimer's to control that part of her. A peace came over her face when she knew the books would be safe.

A couple of weeks later, I contacted Anita and asked if it was a good day to pick up the personal books. Once again I was greeted with a wide open door and a very gentle hug. The carnation flowers were just right. Tom greeted me by saying, "Hi." And together, Winnie, Anita, and I went immediately downstairs. I did not bring enough boxes; however, I was extremely careful in placing the huge amount of books between the boxes so that I didn't damage any of them.

Interestingly, Winnie would quickly hand me books from the shelves. My job was to fill boxes and then take them to my vehicle. Anita would look at a book, pause, and slowly hand it to me. I started to realize the heavy responsibility that Anita had entrusted to me in taking good care of her precious books. I noticed some books on teaching and asked if the family would like to have them. Winnie said, "Take them!" She had already checked with Lynn. "Have JJ take all the books. Otherwise, they will be thrown in the garbage or burned." And Lynn meant it!

After cleaning off the wall filled with countless books, Anita took me to another room by the stairway. There were even more books! She informed me that these books had belonged to her stepfather, and she directed me to take good care of them as well. Where would I place all these additional books? But I promised her I would tend to them.

When all the books were cleared away, Anita slowly walked to my car and reached out her thin arm. With her nimble fingers, she touched several books. Her eyes closed, but her head remained upright. She must have silently wept as she realized this was another door of her life closing. She wanted to control her life, not have Alzheimer's blacken out what she so deeply loved.

Scoreboard

Anita: 7; Alzheimer's: 3

Then Winnie said it was time Anita returned to her love seat. The caretaker started to walk in front of us, but Anita did not walk with Winnie. She stopped, turned around, and looked at me. "Remember me," she said. Then Anita asked Winnie, "Will she come visit me again?"

Winnie heard Anita and told her that this common stranger would surely return to visit her.

I saw a moment that I had never seen before in Anita. She had mentioned this subject before, and I heard what she said; however, this time her eyes looked different. As I took Anita's arm and guided her upstairs, I promised this very special lady that I would never forget her. "Will you come visit me?" Anita whispered again. Winnie heard Anita's first expression of concern but not the second.

"Yes." I whispered and agreed to the request. Winnie gave me a concerned look that still burns in my mind today. I was very humbled that this author had entrusted me with her books and now requested that I continue to visit her. Since that day, I've learned the deep responsibility of a promise. Meanwhile, that familiar smile graced my heart.

After arriving back upstairs, Anita and I visited for just a few more minutes. She spoke about her stepfather's books and how it was good to know they would be safe. *What does she mean by safe?* I wondered. I have treasured the many educational books that Anita used throughout her teaching years. That day the author really became my mentor. To this day, Anita still teaches me about life, cultures, and love through communication. Her precious books are still so filled with life as I read through them.

Winnie's look told me it was time to leave. I said goodbyes and returned home to unload my car, which was filled to the brim with a huge variety of wonderful books, including many in different languages. They were from countries around the world where Anita and Tom had traveled over the years. Anita said she could understand words in about twelve different languages, but she only spoke eight fluently. She mentioned that Tom found it far easier to learn different languages than she did. Back on the day Anita was our guest author, Lynn briefly mentioned how her parents had an uncanny ability to learn languages. They loved traveling around the world. They spoke Spanish, Portuguese, Russian, Italian, German, Japanese, Korean, Chinese, and many others fluently. And here I only spoke English.

Later looking through the books, I noticed the publishing dates. Some books were close to eighty years old. They did not smell, and they were in excellent condition. Others were partial book sets. When I checked their worth for insurance purposes, I found that none had value except the fact that they were Anita's books and teaching collections. When I asked the value at a local library, I was informed to place the samples in the free area located by their front door.

Over the next several weeks, Anita was constantly on my mind. The caregiver phoned and asked if I could come visit my mentor. My hubby and I had an appointment, so I was unable to visit. The next week I contacted the caregiver and asked if it was a good time to visit Anita. She encouraged me to come. Anita's vocabulary was becoming more and more limited. Then before leaving for home, I received even more books. Where would I store them? These books were part of a reference library. It was not a complete set, and the volumes looked well used. I did not question any of this because I did not want to upset Anita. Her attention span was dwindling.

Scoreboard

Anita: 7; Alzheimer's: 4

After our next meeting, I carried two more boxes of books to my car. Books were spread all over this home. Mine was the same now.

Three weeks later it was another very hot summer day, and once again, I wiped the sweat from my brow. Thankfully, I contained the perspiration, and Anita did not need to wipe any drops from my face. Immediately, I was informed there were more books. Was there ever an ending? I thought about Lynn's words, "Take them!" Would I need to disappoint my author and not take any more of her books, or should I just pass them on to a library? After carrying several more boxes of books to my car, I returned to the family home. Suddenly, perspiration poured from my face. Anita motioned for Winnie to bring me a glass of water. I was extremely embarrassed, but I gladly drank the glass of water. I drank it slowly so that I wasn't impolite.

Then my eyes saw a box of magazines that was ready for me to carry to my car. I asked Winnie if any family members wanted them, but she said that Anita needed to get rid of them and that the family did not want any more books or magazines. I understood.

Scoreboard

Anita: 8; Alzheimer's: 4

As I was leaving, my eyes noticed the living room clock. It had been well past twenty minutes. No wonder Winnie wanted me to get out of the family home. I suppose the next day Anita would be hard to handle because all this activity was taking so much of her energy. Or could it actually be that saying goodbye to more of her books produced a sorrowful pain the next day?

Driving home, a poem about life came to my mind. It was fun creating this poem. I call it "Poem of Acceptance." I thought about how and when people met. What types of discussions beyond the weather were generated from general associates that led to people becoming friends? Was there a friendship beginning between Anita and me, or was it something else?

A poem becomes more personal when someone creates their own poetry. Many people probably create their own poems, but this moment in time was only the second time I had written something really from my heart. The first time came when I enter a lyric contest some forty years earlier. I didn't win, but the song were produced and made into a simple record. I still have the record. It was about a friend who had died and how she would be missed. Now here is a poem about life and the value we place on friendships. But was Anita really my friend?

Poem of Acceptance

A smile is a sign of joy.
A hug is a sign of love.
A laugh is a sign of happiness.
Walking together is refreshing.
We will remember each other.
Meanwhile, to have friends like us—
That is just a sign of good taste!
—JJ Janice

Perhaps there is a place hidden in our hearts where we all want to be remembered. Sometimes these precious seasons have an expiration date. These friendships are special and appreciated. Some are long-lasting golden gifts. Then there might be a time period when someone appears for a brief moment but leaves a positive or negative impression. There will always be some special people we instantly forge strong bonds with, walking hand in hand, arm in arm along the journey of life, even if it's only for a short time.

    Selective moments in time are breathtaking. Those special events that we remember always bring continuous smiles to our faces.

Chapter 7

I've Been Waiting for You

My dearest diary, very seldom is there something more uplifting than a good laugh or loving hug. The sound of laughter can for only a moment stir the heart and encourage joy. During the various times I was visiting Anita, only once did I see her laugh. It sounded like a short tune from heaven. Time once again passed quickly. I had forgotten to value important actions like keeping my promise to Anita during my busy life.

It was the beginning of fall, and the trees were filled with beautiful and various colored autumn leaves. The caregiver answered my phone call. She stated that I was not welcome to visit Anita. She ended the slight conversation by including that my good actions in bringing Anita flowers were starting to upset Anita. She was afraid that the vase with water would spill onto the carved table. She didn't want the table to become damaged. I understood.

Our visiting times had been so precious that eliminating them crushed my heart, but perhaps it was time to say goodbye and accept the fact that Alzheimer's was taking over Anita's life.

Weeks passed by, and I remained so upset. Restless nights became more and more frequent. Tears flowed down my cheeks and dropped onto the soft pillow. Some days I started sobbing as I drove by the lake on my way to work. My heart was ripped apart remembering Anita's precious words, "I've been waiting for you."

More than a year earlier when our relationship had started, I was simply meeting an author, but over many visits she had become my mentor. She would greet me with these precious words, "I have been waiting for you." Now these words were haunting my memory night and day.

It was never my intention to overstay my welcome at Anita's home. After all, that front door was wide open, and Anita would always greet me with a smile and a hug. Something just was not right. On the other hand, I needed to accept the fact that her Alzheimer's was advancing. Perhaps Anita would not even remember me or even want me to come visit her. My heart prepared for her not to remember me.

One Saturday afternoon I wrote a thank-you note on a yellow piece of stationery. It had a hilly landscape scene with the sun coming over the mountains. The letter told Anita that some of her books had been sent to schools in Africa. There were many different places to fish in Africa. These books would help teachers enjoy reading English and learn more vocabulary words. Readers would enjoy these extra Texas fishing books and some from Anita's personal library as they glanced at photographs or read a novel from her collection.

What was important was to apologize to Anita for making her so tired. She was to be thanked for offering the very large broken mirror in her basement, but that mirror was actually larger than my car. As for her precious books, it was important for me to thank her again for being so very generous. I verified that the promise to find good homes for each book would be my goal. However, I wanted to keep the bulk of her personal books for my own library.

I was so scared to make the gutsy decision to contact Anita's home again and request to visit her. Winnie thought that Anita would become overly tired if I came and visited. *Should I bring flowers on this next trip or not?* Now this was part of the Alzheimer's that I recognized. My uncle went through this phase as his Alzheimer's had progressed.

Scoreboard

Anita: 8; Alzheimer's: 5

The protective caregiver did not appreciate me phoning for permission to visit Anita. For the first time in my life, I took a stand and put my foot down. I told her I was coming over to give Anita her card. I hung up, got into my car, and drove straight to see Anita, expecting this would be the last time I saw her. There were no flowers purchased, only the homemade card. I knew the caregiver wouldn't welcome me, but what about Anita? Had her Alzheimer's progressed to the point that she no longer recognized me? If so, then my promise to her had been fulfilled, or so I thought. Perhaps the endless sleepless nights would finally become a distant memory.

Arriving at the family home, I saw that Tom wasn't waving to me. I had to knock firmly at the front door several times. The caregiver was in the back kitchen area and didn't hear the knocking. Finally, she came and opened the door. She was very surprised by my forceful words, "I want to see Anita." In fact, her face looked very displeased, and I was surprised but relieved that she didn't phone the police. When the door was cracked slightly open, I insisted, "I really want to see Anita, and I know she wants me to visit her. Besides, I made a homemade card with my apologies for staying so long."

The upset caregiver walked away from the slightly open door. I understood the caregiver needed to protect the health of this Alzheimer's patient. I just needed to know that Anita indeed did not want me around. This would be my closure to a promise I made to a needy lady who didn't want to be forgotten.

I stepped through the partially open front door, which had in the past been a wide open welcome mat. I just wanted to run to my car and weep, but something stopped my feet from moving and blocked the tears from coming. I held my head up and shoulders back. I just *had to know* how she was and apologize for my careless overstaying.

When I entered the living room, I saw Anita was sitting in her usual place on her love seat, reading the newspaper. She looked up and saw me walking toward her. There was that warm smile on her face. She immediately placed the newspaper and her glasses on the coffee table and started to stand up. Our eyes instantly connected. I knew she saw my tears welling up as our eyes met. There was a twinkle in Anita's eyes too. My heart was humbled.

Scoreboard

Anita: 9; Alzheimer's: 5

My mentor was coming to greet me. We hugged for a very long time and held each other so close. Then Anita stared into my soul. With a very soft voice she said, "I have been waiting for you." More tears came to my eyes, and we hugged again. Joy filled my heart. If I had been a burden for staying so long in the past, this wonderful lady had forgiven me, or did she not remember me staying so long?

Anita returned to her love seat. As usual, I went to sit on the green sofa. She moved over and motioned for me to sit beside her. Shyly, I presented the homemade card with the words I had written from my heart. I hoped that it would even become precious to my mentor. Her smile just beamed as I handed the card to her. Then I asked, "Would you like me to read it to you?" Anita nodded her head yes and touched my left hand with her right hand.

Scoreboard

Anita: 10; Alzheimer's: 5

She firmly held on to my hand. We slowly and carefully opened the homemade card. Anita could tell it was homemade because of the stationery. This appeared to please her very much. I now strive to hand-write thank-you notes expressing appreciation as much as possible or at least email people how much they are appreciated.

Together, we held the yellow paper firmly. Her hand did not even quiver. I read the words out loud, slightly observing Anita's facial expressions. She smiled that warm smile and even nodded her head as she tried to look at the words my finger pointed out. I read very slowly in complete sentences. I figured she still really wanted me to be part of her life. Now I understood there is a deeper meaning of the word *promise*. When a person makes a promise, I think his or her subconscious mind remembers the promise and holds that word as a commitment. Such action can bring some sleepless nights.

The caregiver came in and asked what we were doing. I told her that I helped Anita open the homemade card, and together, we were reading it. I handed the caregiver the card. Instead of handling it back to us, she walked away with the card. This irritated me because I had not finished reading the card. Anita just kept looking at the caregiver as she left the room. Was this an indication that I was done and it was time to leave even though I had just arrived? This caregiver meant well, but why didn't she pass the card back to Anita and me? I respected her responsibilities and promised the caregiver I would be leaving in a few minutes.

I think the caregiver noticed that Anita's hand was clamped onto mine; not mine to hers.

It was time to leave. I asked Anita for permission to say Hello and Goodbye to Tom, who was watching an opera on TV. Anita motioned for me to help her up from the love seat. Together, we very slowly walked arm in arm to the TV room. When we entered, Tom looked our way and said, "Why, hello!"

As Anita and Tom looked at each other, they gave off sparks of love and happiness. Anita sat down in her rocker. I popped my head through the back kitchen area to alert the caregiver I was leaving.

Tom asked why I was leaving so soon. My heart sank when I heard his precious words. Then I turned to Anita, who was watching as Tom and I spoke. I knelt down beside her rocking chair and looked into her eyes. She turned her head more toward me, and then slowly, she looked up to the ceiling. The most beautiful laughter came from her.

This happy sound brought the caregiver hurrying into the doorway to see what was happening. The caregiver noticed me giving

Anita a slight kiss, and Anita kissed me back. I believe God made cheeks for smiles and kisses.

Immediately, the caregiver walked me to the front door. As I opened it and stepped out, the caregiver said, "You are really something." I'm still not totally sure what she meant because I was only concerned about keeping a promise. It is the only time I stopped by to visit Anita in her home without asking permission first.

Had Anita's prayer come true? I know God heard my prayer. She must have prayed for me to stop by and visit her. Why else was I having so many sleepless nights and feeling pressured to make that phone call for weeks? If there was any offense, she had forgiven me. I was elated that my mentor had remembered me and who I was to her. The welcome invitation remained open so I could return and step inside this loving family's home and continue growing closer to them. Those words still ring in my ears. *I have been waiting for you.* My commitment would continue until Alzheimer's totally took over her memory. Meanwhile, Anita had had the last laugh.

Scoreboard

Anita: 11; Alzheimer's: 5

Later that evening I contacted Lynn and inquired if there had been any issues in regard to visiting her mother. She told me how I had been able to bring out what she could not, keeping her mother's mind alert and the memories restored as best as possible. This gave me some peace of mind and confidence that I had made the right decision to go with my gut instinct. That night I had a very relaxing and peaceful night's sleep.

I had learned my lesson. Do not stay long visiting a person who is sick or has a disease even when the person wants you to remain longer. That person might become overly tired the next day. If Anita would not have recognized me, it would have been her Alzheimer's, and I would have slipped out of her life; however, the time would remain in my memory.

Chapter 8

The Questions

Before leaving the family home on the previous visit, I asked this gracious author if she would like me to bring anything to her. She informed me that I spent too much money on flowers. Anita remembered the flowers. I asked her if the flowers brought her happiness. Anita responded that they made her husband and her happy. Thus, I closed the subject, and I continued bringing her beautiful floral arrangements. However, she never mentioned to me that she was deeply concerned that the flower vase filled with water might tip over and harm the homemade wood-carved piece. I'm grateful that the caregiver brought this to my attention. When people move from old to elderly, what can bring some happiness into their lives? Family, of course, brings happiness, but what else? That is simple. For my mentor it was having some beautiful fresh flowers to greet her for a few days.

Several visits earlier I kept asking myself, "Is she the one?" I often wondered what the caregiver meant and why Anita said, "Yes." Perhaps there was more to the yes than obtaining books. Anita had to trust that I would keep her books safe, and eventually, I did dismiss the statement.

A couple of weeks later when I was visiting Anita and Tom, they asked me a direct question. That profound question still lingers in my mind. Anita looked straight at me and said that Tom and she had discussed my nickname "Book Lady," which stunned me.

I was just a simple common stranger visiting two elderly people. What would they have spoken together about me? Then I smiled to myself. Perhaps the question would be about education or books. Both people had a very serious look on their faces. "What would you like to ask me?" I inquired.

Anita motioned for Tom to ask the question, "What does money mean to you?" That was easy to answer, but what a funny question to ask. I looked at each of them and carefully replied, "Money? Money can be used for good or bad. You can control money and enjoy the benefits of using it wisely, or you can waste it." I continued talking about how sometimes money can end up controlling your life like it often does through drugs or shopping. Life is easier when a person is blessed with money and uses it for good like traveling or helping others. This elderly couple appeared to accept my answer about the good and bad ways of handling money. Both looked at each other, and that family smile appeared on both of their faces.

Then it was my turn to ask this couple a question. Anita and Tom were surprised as I inquired, "If you were given any gift, what would you like?" Tom immediately said he wanted some wine from France or perhaps Italy, depending on what he was eating. Anita hesitated and then quietly spoke. She wanted the ability to communicate the thoughts and words in her brain like she had before.

I have often thought of the two differences. One wanted the pleasure of taste, perhaps bringing back happy memories when the family lived or traveled years earlier. The other person wanted to reach out to retrieve verbal communication. I recalled how important communication truly was, even if only through looks.

When I had my own daycare and preschool, all it took was just a look to let a child know right and wrong. I did not speak much to adults because my sentences were constantly interrupted by children's activities. It was a great time to help train these small children to listen. It was a fun time educating children to think on their own and express their thoughts. Now I was reminded of the importance of words for communication purposes. Even as an instructor, I knew the importance of communication, yet the word appears to be taken for granted most of the time. Everyone assumes everyone else is on the same wave length about the dictionary's meaning of words. One person can connect on a subject while the other person is speaking on a total different level of understanding. To communicate is essential. However, there can always be a miscommunication even when a person thinks one is communicating. A prime example is about the flowers being appreciated, but in reality, it was the water that was upsetting Anita.

Sometimes we cannot understand or relate to what another person's heart goes through. An example was when Anita had mentioned Lynn's lifestyle. Lynn's early wild lifestyle had ended a good thirty years earlier, but it hadn't ended for Anita.

During one conversation I asked Anita if it was okay for me to pursue a friendship with Lynn. Why did I request her permission? Why would I even want Lynn's friendship? Anita angrily spit out, "She does not know what I have gone through for her." This parent probably went through humiliation and embarrassment for her daughter.

Driving home, I stopped and parked at a grocery store and sat in the car, thinking about my past. I hadn't done this for years. But why now? This mentor of mine sure could stir up deep thoughts that had been buried for years. I didn't cry. I just sat and thought.

I *kind of* understood what Anita meant. I put my parents through a hard time when they paid for my college. My parents worked very hard in order to make ends meet and to save as much as possible. Being a teenager, I really expected my parents to pay for college. I never thought about household finances or the daily, weekly, and monthly costs to raise a family. It did not dawn on me how much money was needed to really pay for other things beyond college tuition, such as books, food, travel, housing, supplies, and fun activities. I knew the tuition price, but the reality of true college costs wasn't part of my comprehension. Growing older, my mind needed time to understand that I needed to be on my own, but it took me a long time to understand adulthood. I lived in my own silent world and didn't comprehend other peoples' expenses. My mind went back in time.

I remembered how the last summer before graduating must have been an extreme hardship for my parents and family. There was a sum of thirty-two dollars left to pay off on the tuition for my graduating year. I remembered my mother informing the college that it was my responsibility to pay the rest of the tuition because I had not worked enough hours on the farm. Why did she have to tell them that I hadn't worked long enough hours pulling weeds in the strawberry field? I never was good with my hands, and I cleaned thousands of eggs, only breaking a few. I tried my best to make my parents proud. My fingers never did pick berries or beans very fast. It was so embarrassing when younger pickers earned more money than me. I must have been an embarrassment to my parents too.

Then I thought about the weekend when I traveled home and enjoyed Mom's delicious fried chicken, homemade potato salad and pies, plus the fresh garden vegetables. Before leaving our house that weekend, I realized there was only thirty-five cents in my pocket. When I asked my mom if she had a dollar because I only had enough money for the bus to arrive at school, she informed me that I should have planned better. She gave me no money. From that day onward, I made sure I paid for everything when my parents came to visit our home or when we were visiting them in Nebraska. But the guilt lingered beyond my parents. I began paying for friends' food when we went out. If I saw that someone needed something, I would go out and even pay for one of their educational quarters. For years I lived with the thought I needed to help others because I was not good enough to be helped in my time of need. If I saw a need, even a person who needed a simple pencil or some notebook paper, I stepped up to the plate and silently helped fill their needs. I didn't need to be recognized. Just to help others brings a joy to my heart.

To this day it is very hard to allow anyone to pay or give me something. Why should I *still* feel so guilty because I spent my parents' hard-earned money for college? It's still a thorn in my subconscious. Perhaps with both of my parents gone, I really needed to forgive myself and say to my subconscious, "It's okay *not* to pay out so much to help other people." I thought back to the last time I purchased shoes, clothes, jewelry, makeup, or something for myself, even like new glasses? Well, I do love going out to lunch with friends and enjoying wonderful food and conversations. It's not always healthy to think about other people's needs because sometimes the person doesn't appreciate the extra meal you've ordered for them to take home. I am a human being too.

 I thought about the pros and cons to Lynn's life and how it affected her parents. Perhaps we had more in common than I thought. Maybe that was why my subconscious requested permission from Anita to become part of Lynn's life. All people make mistakes, and no one should point fingers at anyone, especially those whose lives have changed for the good. People should take out their own log from their life instead of throwing stones at the less fortunate or whoever they disagree with on any subject. Well, that's my attitude.

 Material things can be replaced with other material things; however, holding tight to another hand, a warm smile coming from the depths of another person's heart, or even a kind word, especially those from hand-written notes, becomes priceless. My mentor was filling an empty space in my life by challenging me.

 As time passed, Anita and I became closer. A person can ask, "How does a person with Alzheimer's become a mentor? How can that person teach or show anyone anything when he or she is in the last stage of Alzheimer's?" It is easy. It is called love. Maybe it comes from prayers too. The person's heart repents, and faith comes alive. Ask what you will and know God the Father will see your heart's deepest desires is so very true. Perhaps realizing the desire to be loved can be perceived in another person's heart. Is this what Anita was passing on to me, or was it what she observed in looking through my eyes into my heart? Perhaps it was her need? To fulfill a need, sometimes a bad thought or action is blocking future happiness. There is a difference between repentance and remorse. To repent means to totally change, but to have a remorseful attitude means to apologize without any change. The person is only sorry because he or she was caught. Meanwhile, what did Anita perceive in me that I needed help with changing in my attitude?

I thought about a conversation I had with Lynn when we talked about our moms. I understood to some degree where she was coming from because of my own mother's past criticisms of me as a field worker. This had a lasting impact on my life. In other words, I perceived that I was not able to put in a good day's work for pay. Anyway, as for me, I always wondered if that was the division between my own mother and me. Thinking back, I do not remember having one long conversation with either of my parents at any time during my life. This was totally opposite with Lynn communicating with her parents.

The subconscious holds everything from the moment we are conceived till death. What does anyone's subconscious really hold locked away deep in our gray matter?

Lynn explained how she believed that once a creative thought became a desire, it could eventually fill a void in a person's heart. Then after time the thought becomes a belief that eventually can turn into reality. She informed me she appreciated me helping her mother, but she wanted to warn me to please stay away from her papa.

I constantly informed Lynn that Anita was her mother and I had my own parents. But where was Anita's love for Lynn? Life can give some real serious blows that can crush anyone's heart at times, but nothing compared to Lynn's deeply hurting heart.

Now, my dearest diary, looking back, I believe that my dearest mother loved me. However, perhaps she could not see my potential talents. She could not see that these hands were meant for teaching or even writing to you in this book.

Chapter 9

Asking for Help

The fall season passed quickly. The wet cold weather sneakily kept attacking my health. I had the flu followed by several colds that my body could not shake. Here's the actual fact I needed to face. I didn't remember Anita for weeks at a time. Then suddenly, it would happen again. A promise is a promise, and that fact lingered in my mind between Christmas and New Year's. I knew I was not family; however, there was something connecting Anita and me. Why did she ask me to remember her? She had her own family, and so did I. Something within myself was becoming more and more frustrated thinking about Anita.

Our paths must have met before, but where and when? I forced myself to think and reason as my heart raced. Why was my heart suddenly drawn back to Anita?

That extremely strong impulse kept knocking on my mind, so finally, I caved during the late happy holiday season, especially around New Year's Day, which was coming soon. Should I email Lynn, or should I phone Anita? My thoughts were so wishy-washy. If I only contact one of them, this uneasy exercise would be over, and I could move forward to the new year's responsibilities.

I asked myself if I had forgotten the deep meaning of the word promise. A promise is like a vow or oath. I wondered if this was why I was thinking about Anita. I didn't mean to forget Anita and not visit her, but I didn't want to take my bad health to her home. I questioned if Lynn would recognize my email address. Would she even respond? How silly of me. Of course, Lynn would not be waiting for me to contact her. Would she remember walking arm in arm at her parents' home almost a year earlier? It brought a warm smile to my face, remembering Anita's last birthday.

It was time to make a decision to keep my promise or move on with my family's lives.

Message dated 12/28/06 9:37 AM (partial email)

I trust you are still enjoying the "snow" for a little while longer... How are you and your loved ones doing? Last night I woke up dreaming about giving your dad some homemade cookies. I saw your mom with flowers. I haven't seen them since you were on vacation... I promised your mom that I would not "forget her." She was very concerned to be remembered and asked if I would be visiting her again. The last time I saw your mother I held her hand and told her how soft her hands were and how beautiful her nails looked. She looked at mine and asked me if I worked outside in the yard. I do not like yard work. I like admiring other people, like you, who enjoy yard work. Of course, my hands are very dry because I seldom use hand creams and my nails are the pits. How are your parents? ... and how are you? You remain in my thoughts and prayers. Take good care and be safe with the snow and icy weather. If you have a few extra minutes after grocery shopping, please stop by and we'll enjoy some laughs. Warmly, JJ

Message dated 12/28/06 11:31 AM (partial email)

I have some sad news, nobody died, relax ... but three weeks ago my mother fell and broke her hip. She is at a convalescent center. Her Alzheimer's has gotten very, very bad. I went to see her on Xmas day, and she didn't know me. All she could do was "babble."

JJ Janice

I'm afraid she's lost her mind. The doctor said because of this she probably won't be able to do the rehab necessary to walk again. She just doesn't understand. We might not be bringing her home. If she's just "bedbound" we can put a hospital bed in the front room, but she has to stay in it and her Alzheimer's might not allow that. It's so sad. They made her a bed on the floor, because she keeps trying to get up. I cried. Thank you for your kind email, perhaps someday you could visit her? She's in room 100. She's been asking people to help her kill herself… THIS SUCKS! … THERE IS NO DIGNITY IN DEATH… it's killing me to see her like this. Sorry for the "uncheery" news… Lynn

Message dated 12/28/06 4:39 PM (partial email)

Hi Lynn,

…just returned from seeing your mom. She was on the floor sleeping and the light was off. I knelt beside her and let her know that JJ was here to say hello and asked if I could brush her hair… she was still as I started to gently brush her hair… on the third stroke her eyes opened slowly… I promised that I would return tomorrow. The head nurse came in and asked if I was her daughter. I replied simply, "No, I'm Lynn's friend and Anita's Book Lady." I reached into my back jean pocket to show her your email. She told me to stay as long as I wanted. I know she liked to read newspapers and books. Next time I visit your mother I will bring a newspaper for her. JJ

    (At times I just could not tell Lynn the truth that her mother recognized me.)
    (It is not good to lie! But how could have I told Lynn that her mother recognized me?)
    Lynn replied the next day with a snippy email.

Entwined Hearts

Message dated 12/29/06 9:28 AM (Partial email)

My mother has not been able to read for over two years! She pretends she's reading words! Lynn

Scoreboard

Anita: 11; Alzheimer's: 6

Starting the New Year was like renewing my promise to Anita to remember her. Several days during the first week, I would check up on her and report back to Lynn in the evenings. I knew Lynn visited her father once or twice a week. She would drive him to the center to visit his wife of seventy years. It was absolutely heart-wrenching when Lynn told me about how her mother sometimes screamed at her papa and her to get out of the room.

Over the next few weeks, the doors of friendship through communications opened wider between Lynn and me. There were so many emotions Lynn was going through that there were times I wanted to push the delete button. It was heartbreaking to realize the defeat of a person's mind because of Alzheimer's. I knew very little about this memory-stealing disease, but I was learning fast to a small degree what this family must have been experiencing with Alzheimer's. I noticed this vibrant lady's personality and her body's strength diminishing.

Lynn's emails felt like a wild volcano that just waited to fully erupt. Anyone else like her I would have refused further contact, but Lynn's uncontrollable emotions somehow appeared to pull us closer. Nonetheless, Lynn's ups and downs disturbed me. Was this part of what Alzheimer's relatives faced within the family? Each member must have gone through this agonizing time in their own ways. Could I handle this new support role much longer when I had dodged these times in the past?

My thoughts raced. What was proper for an outsider since I was not a relative? I just kindly told a lonely lady that I would remember her. I took this commitment very seriously. Be aware of the words a person speaks. Your subconscious will hold you accountable. More than liked, I looked forward to visiting Anita even in her declining condition. Well, my dearest diary, reality continued as I dealt with Anita's Alzheimer's. I needed to make sure that all of my own commitments were taken care of—my husband, family, friends, work, and volunteering—before visiting Anita. It was my choice to help Anita, and Lynn became a happy part of my life. Each thought of precious Lynn and especially Anita still brings a smile to my face years later.

God must have heard Anita's prayers. Someone else must have been chosen to come into Anita's declining last stage of Alzheimer's. But who chose to not get involved or not come help as part of this family? He must have finally given up and looked around. He picked me. Actually, it was refreshing being with Anita. She had become my mentor, even with her health condition. My mentor, an Alzheimer's patient, taught me the value of forgiveness and patience, and she showed me it was okay to be challenged. Perhaps I needed to learn to forgive. Many years later I had a picture of my aura taken. It was colored with loads of greens and yellows with a little red and purple. The lady who took the aura picture said that I was filled with love. Well, sometimes that's true.

Again, I started believing that Anita was scared and lonely within herself and fearful of dying alone. She was probably questioning if there was life after death. She had no control over her future. Eternal life is for every person whether it is believed or not. There is life after death here on earth. About two weeks before Anita passed away, I told her about my experience of heaven and what I believed.

"Anita, many years ago I went to the hospital to have a bone spur removed from my hand. It was supposed to be an in-and-out surgery that should have taken about three hours total. However, I was given too much anesthesia. For about fifteen minutes, I was transported through a black hole to a place where the light was so bright that even the sun looked dull, but it didn't hurt my eyes. It was an extremely peaceful sphere. A soft voice asked me, 'Would you like to see Jesus?' I thought for a moment and answered, 'No, I want to see our children grow up.'

"This sphere was so peaceful. Immediately, I was transported back to the operating table. The rest of the morning and all afternoon and even into the evening time, I slept. Suddenly, waking up late in the evening, I realized the peaceful place was gone. I really wanted to return back to it. Then I remembered I wanted to see our kids grow up. I immediately requested for the staff to contact my hubby so that he could pick me up and take me home. I didn't tell anyone about my experience because no one would have believed me.

"For days I longed to return to that peaceful place. I would shut my eyes, but returning to that sphere didn't happen. It only remained in my soul (mind, will, and emotions). God the Father is good because every person has the privilege to believe in Jesus as their Savior or not. Now I know without a doubt I can look up at the big blue sky and the night sky engulfed with stars and literally know that beyond what my eyes can view is a peaceful sphere and a real heaven. Knowing there is a real heaven tells me there is a real hell."

Anita knew she was dying, and telling her about my heavenly experience appeared to give her some peace of mind. Even Lynn noticed her mother's peacefulness visiting her that next week. I thought perhaps Anita must have been a silent prayer warrior who had a connection between God Almighty and our hearts. This understanding has been hard for me to digest. I'm not special. I'm just a common stranger.

For the next couple of weeks, Anita's health continued declining. She was fading away to almost nothing. One afternoon I noticed Anita was propped up in her bed, holding a picture of Lynn. I placed my finger on Anita's forehead and gave the sign of the cross. A power came upon me, and I stated to her, "In the name of the Father, Son, and Holy Spirit, you are Mine!" Then I quietly spoke, "I love you," and gently kissed her forehead.

That evening before Anita went to sleep, I wanted to drive to the center to verify Anita would pass away that night or the next day. As my car approached the nearby street, there was a stoplight.

JJ Janice

My steering wheel would not turn toward the center. It's the honest truth! I tried another route, but as I turned toward the center, my car drove independent of me. It would not comply with my direction.

I recalled another time when this type of situation happened. I was traveling alone and approaching the freeway entrance when my car literally pulled over to the side of the road. I put my foot down on the gas, but nothing happened. The car would not move. My eyes viewed a hitchhiker through the mirror. No way was I going to pick up anyone needing a ride. After a few seconds, I got out of my car and asked if he would like some water. The man graciously nodded his head yes. Instead of walking over and kindly handing the water bottle to him, I threw it at him. Then disgustedly, I returned to my car, expecting to drive away. The engine started, but that car would not move.

Once again, I got out of my car and asked the man if he was hungry. Then I proceeded to get an apple and threw it at him again. Of course, he caught both the water bottle and the apple. Suddenly, I blurted out, "Would you like a ride?" A smile came upon his face. We located a small open space for his backpack. He saw my cooler on the front seat, so I asked him if he was hungry. For more than a hundred miles, this man slowly ate and drank everything I had.

When he was through eating and drinking, he commented, "Do you normally pick up hitchhikers?"

I replied, "No."

A few miles down the road, he started to look around the inside of the vehicle and asked in a low tone, "Do you have a gun in here?"

I responded, "It doesn't matter if I have a gun. What matters is I know how to use one." I thought the man was going to open the passenger door and jump out of our moving car. He was the hitchhiker, not me. I should be the person scared of him. That day the angels were in charge. My attitude didn't matter because they would keep me safe. Lynn started to laugh because she loved guns. "I know how to use one too."

When we arrived at the truck station, I handed him a ten-dollar bill. He told me that he was traveling to the East Coast to take care of his mother, who had been beaten up by her boyfriend. He planned to harm the man who had hurt his mother. After listening to my Christian music, he changed his mind and would only hurt him a little. It amazes me how God Almighty sends His angels down to connect people. When I told this story to Lynn, she said, "I'm not sure about believing in God and angels." I just looked at Lynn and smiled because everyone needs to make up their own minds about what they believe.

Chapter 10

The Center

My dearest diary, I want to take you back to the beginning when I visited Anita at the convalescent center. Circumstances prompted me to eventually see Anita twice every day. This three-month period among mother, daughter, and common stranger generated many emotions and changes in all three of our lives. There were various experiences with Lynn that I tolerated. Over time I realized most of her stress involved her mother's Alzheimer's disease. I will tell you my experiences in several parts.

Part 1

On a very cold afternoon just before New Year's Day, I drove up to the convalescent center's entrance. Surprisingly, there was an open parking space right near the center's front door. I have good luck with parking spaces. If I'm supposed to be somewhere, there will be an open parking space near the front door. Thus, I knew I was where I was meant to be at the right time.

Slowly walking toward the double front doors, I observed everything possible. My mind flashed back in history when I received a warm greeting and a gentle but firm hug from Anita at the family home. Now this double door automatically opened wide, but no one greeted me. I was really anxious yet afraid to enter the center through these doors. It would open up a new world of experiences, and I wasn't sure how to handle the future.

I understood about senior citizens' residences because that was where my mother resided. She was very happy with her center. She had her hair done up each week, and her fingernails were beautiful. She loved socializing with the variety of people from different backgrounds. She even enjoyed the meals with laughter and conversations. But my knowledge of a convalescent center was mostly lacking.

The center's information booth was closed. The halls were a solemn place. No music played in the background. My nostrils searched for the smell of fresh flowers in the air, yet I could detect nothing. The center took pride in cleanliness because there were no odors through the hallway.

The walls had many wonderful nature paintings. The center even had a reading area with a lit fireplace. I slowly strolled back down the same hallway, trying to locate a nurses' station.

My feet located a fork in the hallway. I needed to decide which hallway to walk down. "Okay, God, send Your angels. Show me the correct hallway because I am lost," I said. God does answer prayers, sometimes instantly. I chose to turn right, and at the end of this hallway, I found a nurses' reception station. I inquired about Anita and requested the location of room 100.

The head nurse was very patient, explaining how she had to register my name. Then she pointed to another hallway close by where Anita's room was located. Slowly, my feet took one step at a time. It was time to face reality, and that reality was hard to swallow. The room's number was right there in front of me. My feet stood still. I gazed upon the nameplate.

My eyes started to fill with water once again, thinking back, knowing the last time it was Anita who greeted me with totally open arms at her home's front door. Those precious times had ended, and I needed to accept this change. It was hard for me to accept, but it must have been devastating for family members. These family members confronted this harsh reality and went through years of watching

JJ Janice

Alzheimer's take away a vibrant wife and mother. Their footsteps were much heavier than mine. My thoughts returned to the resident's nameplate and how many other families went through this horror.

Now it was my turn to open my arms. Would this mentor remember me? Would she even want me or anyone to visit her? Would my promise to Anita be forgotten now? What about Lynn? Lynn was totally crushed when she wasn't recognized. How much longer could she take the devastating disease destroying her mother?

I held my head up, threw my shoulders back, smiled, and stepped toward Anita's new world. The shock of seeing her bed empty pierced my heart. She was not in it. Then sudden relief came as I recalled what Lynn had emailed me.

On the other side of the hospital bed, a mattress laid on the floor. Anita was lying below the closed window. Even with the blinds closed, there was cool air flowing over my mentor. The lights were off. Her very frail body was crouched over with no blanket covering her. Where was some soft music? There was no symphony music in the background. Anita was used to this type of music because Tom was always playing music from around the world, especially symphony music. She was used to opening the blinds and allowing the sunlight to engulf the room. This atmosphere brought nothing to remind her of her past environments. It reminded me of a dungeon with no sunlight or warmth. Could she return to the family home where she was so used to the past routines? Did no one at the center understand the power of music and light?

I bent down and touched her cold shoulder and very quietly said, "JJ is here." There was no movement. I spoke the same words again and again. I took the brush and gently brushed her hair. After a few seconds, she turned her head slightly toward me. Her eyes opened a crack, but they did not have much life. Did my warm hand on her cold body and gently brushing her hair help Anita know someone was with her? For a fourth time, I mentioned my name again. She appeared to slowly recognize it. Anita started to greet me with a very weak, soft voice, "I have been waiting for you." I only wished Lynn would have been there to know her mother could actually speak in a very slow but whole sentence. Lynn would never have believed these precious moments, but how would she have reacted to those precious words.

Scoreboard

Anita: 12; Alzheimer's: 6

My ears did hear her slow, weak voice speak. I just smiled at Anita's beautiful face. "Hello, Anita. Yes, JJ is here. You are not forgotten." These words brought a slight grin to her lovely face.

Scoreboard

Anita: 13; Alzheimer's: 6

I asked her how she was doing with her broken hip. She didn't respond. Was she listening to her therapist, who told her to exercise and to put pressure on her hip? I mentioned to Anita that this would help her walk again and be somewhat independent. She tried to answer with simple words, but then she just started babbling. The simple words came when she slowed down her words. The babbling happened when she rushed her thoughts. I asked her to speak very slowly so her words were completely understandable. She listened and understood because she slowed down her speech patterns.

As I gazed upon her beautiful face, I was shocked when I noticed there was really only one wrinkle that had started to form between her eyebrows. I almost laughed out loud, realizing she had only one wrinkle compared to my many. Maybe she was in some sort of pain. I asked Anita if she would like her hair brushed some more. Slowly, she blinked her eyes with a very slight nod. So I took the soft hairbrush and very gently brushed her beautiful pure white hair again.

"Anita, you do not even have one wrinkle on your face." I told her how I wished I did not have wrinkles. My wrinkles were the cause of smiling and whistling since I had been a little girl, which had given me whistling lips so that I looked like a fish seeking food. Plus I drank too many sodas throughout my life. All that sugar increased my facial wrinkles too. Even in Anita's physical condition, this author and mentor appeared to be listening attentively. She always did have acute hearing.

I added, "You must have taken very good care of your skin all of your life." She slightly smiled and reached out her nimble hand to mine. Then clearly, she repeated in a weak voice, "I have been waiting for you." Then she said one word, "Water."

"You have drunk a lot of water all of your life?" I inquired. Her eyes started to show some life. I told her I understood what she was saying because I had read that water helped the skin look refreshed.

Then the thought crossed my mind that maybe I really did misunderstand the word water. Perhaps Anita was asking for some water. So I asked if she would like a drink of water. She instantly slurred, "Yes." She didn't pronounce the whole word, but I understood as she blinked her eyes. I located a pink water sponge, wetted it, and gave Anita some water. She was extremely thirsty, and after five sips she felt more comfortable. There was a peaceful look on Anita's face.

I mentioned it was a very nice sunny day. I asked if she would like the blinds open to let in the sunshine. Perhaps it would warm up the room too. So I pulled up the blinds, and it appeared to make Anita happier. Next, I asked her if she would like to lie down in her bed. I could call for help in lifting her up so that we would not fall. I had noticed that a soft cool breeze still kept blowing right over Anita. I glanced around the bed area and didn't see a blanket to put over her cold body.

A few minutes later, an attendant arrived. She explained that Anita had been placed on the floor with a mattress because she kept trying to get out of bed and she was at risk of hurting herself. It was for Anita's own safety to remain on the floor. I inquired about a light blanket to place on top of Anita because of the breeze from the window. There were no light throw blankets available. Besides, Anita would be going to supper soon. I remained for about fifteen minutes and then gave Anita a light hug and told her I would be back the next day.

My mind raced backward, noticing she was wearing the same clothes I saw her wear in her home. There was dried food on her blouse. I also observed that Anita's fingernails were dirty. I would need to visit Anita every day of the week if necessary to make sure the center's employees understood Anita was to wear clean clothes every day. I would help change her clothes if I had to.

Hopefully, I would not ever need to take this action because it might be embarrassing for Anita. After all, I was not a family member or a hired helper. I didn't understand why her fingernails were dirty though. Lynn needed to explain this information to me. I could imagine Lynn just shaking her head as she explained cleanliness.

Part 2

A couple of days later at lunchtime, I joined Anita's table. I did not eat but saw what food she was supposed to consume. Anita wore clean clothes, and her fingernails were clean now too. That was a good move on the center's part. Anita did not want the food. I didn't blame her. It was finely mashed green peas, mashed potatoes, and something else mashed. Perhaps it was chicken, but it was still hard for her to eat. Was Anita supposed to feed herself?

Perhaps she could gum her food, but she was so weak. How could she swallow? How could she do this when she had become even frailer and hardly had any strength? I tried to encourage her to eat, but I would not have eaten that bland food either, not unless I was super hungry.

I remembered my own mother not having teeth and being given very plain food. She tried to gum down the food, but I saw my mom look around the table, locate some milk and pour a little bit of milk on the top of the food so it was easier to swallow. Anita had good strong teeth, but she no longer had the ability to swallow. She had lost the ability to swallow almost two years earlier, so why was she served this type of food? However, she could chew the finely ground food that could eventually slide down her throat.

Scoreboard

Anita: 13; Alzheimer's: 7

Several days later when I went to attend lunch with Anita again, I noticed she had been returned to her bed by twelve thirty. Reading the monthly luncheon sheet, I noticed the listed menu was not the same she had received days earlier.

I decided to see Anita at different times on a daily basis. I would come in the afternoon and in the evening. Dropping in to see Anita at any time during the day or evenings, including weekends, was easy since I lived so close. Mornings were reserved for daily health preparations like bathing and exercising, so I knew it would not be good to stop by the center at that time. Arriving in the afternoon and evenings, I could gather how the staff was caring for Anita.

The center thought I was part of the family. I stressed to them that Anita was my *mentor* and Lynn was my *friend*. Lynn needed help knowing what was happening with her mother, so I would stop by and check up on Anita's condition every day. Lynn lived about an hour and a half away and worked full time, so it was hard for her to see her mother several times a week.

Every evening around nine thirty, I would email Lynn and report about Anita. The following email included a lunchtime experience:

Message dated 1/6/07 10:13 PM (Partial email)

Today I joined your mother at lunchtime. Her eyes were closed. There was food on her plate. I told Anita that I was there and asked her if she would like some food. I gently rubbed her hand and eventually she opened her eyes. I asked her again if she would like some food. She started to open her mouth and the assistant placed a full tablespoon of food in her partially opened mouth. Your mother gagged, but her lips were closed so no food protruded out. She kept choking. Little by little the mouth full of food separated and became moist enough to slither down her throat.

I do not understand why she was given mashed food when you mentioned she couldn't swallow. Does the center understand your mother no longer has the ability to swallow food? While living at home she received healthy liquids that went down her throat easily. Just thought you wanted to know that I did not say anything to anyone. I know I am interfering in your family. I just do not like your mother being treated this way or anyone else being treated in this manner.

Your mother now likes the pink swabs that absorb water. I asked her if she would like some water and she nodded, "Yes."

Notes are taken about what she says so you know our conversations apply towards reality or babbling. When she speaks extremely slowly the word or words can be understood, but most of the time she babbles. Her skin looks better. Her fingernails are cleaner. I usually comb her hair.

Did I ever tell you that I worked at a nursing home for just a few months while attending college? I just could not take seeing wonderful, elderly people disrespected. I would like to think I am thick-skinned, but it broke part of my heart working in these conditions. I admire people who specialize in the health field. They sure do care about people. Hope this does not happen to your mother. Sorry for being hurtful to you. I guess I am just outspoken at times. I will write you tomorrow evening and update you on my visits. Hope you can get some rest. JJ

Ten days later the stress was coming through even stronger in Lynn's email. It sounded like someone who needed a shoulder.

JJ Janice

Message dated 1/16/07 9:41 AM (Partial email)

Nobody should have to live like this. It is terribly depressing. I do not know how much more I can take. It is making me crazy. I LOVE MY BEAR! The homemade quilts are gorgeous also. It touched my heart when you said they were for "people who were hurting." Yes, I am hurting. I have to go to work. I believe I will strap my bear into the passenger seat and he can ride with me. I need a name. I am working on it. I will make a "him" or a "her." It will come to me eventually. By the way, I rode home with my new teddy bear on my lap. I used to make fun of adults and their bears... This is crazy?

My mother never wanted to live like this. I have lung problems from all my stupid years of smoking. I cannot afford an infection with my new tattoo. What do I do? I feel so lost at times. Getting my father to see mom is actually a major hassle for me. I have a very bad back. I was so relieved when he told me yesterday, "We do not need to do this every week." It is terribly depressing. Lynn

My dearest diary, as we continued to communicate through emails, Lynn started to realize there were emotional connections between her mother and me. Lynn could read between the lines. So many times I just could not tell Lynn that her mother would welcome me and together we would use very simple words or sentences to communicate. I would read the local newspaper, magazines, or children's books. Maybe the book would be filled with jokes or simple stories like the ones in the *Reader's Digest*. Later I realized that Anita liked the *Reader's Digest* perhaps because she loved *words* and the short human interest stories. Anyway, it was pleasing to know I had chosen a simple reading magazine with sometimes humorous stories and not just the travel magazines.

Anita would not speak with Lynn. She just babbled. Was Anita rushing through her words with Lynn and Tom? Was her communication processing too fast? She wasn't saying anything that seemed to make sense. More than one time, Anita screamed at Lynn and Tom, "Leave! Get out of here!" Tom was devastated.

Now I understood why Lynn would become so upset visiting her mother. She never knew what type of response her mother would give when they were visiting.

Lynn knew her mother wanted to return home. I've heard this from various other family members and caregivers dealing with Alzheimer's. The Alzheimer's patients want to leave their live-in centers and seek ways to escape in order to return to their homes. According to Lynn, her father, the caregiver, the caregiver's employer, and she went back and forth about the depressing decision to have Anita remain at the center or return Anita to her home. It took a lot of inner fortitude and teamwork to come together and decide Anita should remain where she was currently staying. She would need specialized care during her last stage of Alzheimer's. Besides, Lynn mentioned the family home was much quieter without Anita. Perhaps the hallucination of seeing a line of people pounding on the family door was not in Anita's mind at the center. Lynn said she even screamed at her mother and told her to "shut up" and then told her that there were no people at the front door.

I remember a dear friend telling me how her father thought there was a snake in his home. The family would take him around each room and show him the snake had left. How compassionate!

I was so very proud of this family. It must have broken their hearts, but Lynn said her mother was peaceful now at the center. According to Lynn, Anita had become very hard to handle, another verification that she was in the last stage of Alzheimer's.

Meanwhile, visiting Anita in the evenings remained our private time. She would sit in her wheelchair parked in the nurses' station lobby. Most of the time she spoke very slowly but clearly, "I have been waiting for you." It was like she memorized the words over and over and over again. Her words constantly humbled my heart. She would reach out her feeble hand and place it over mine. Sometimes our hands did not part for a good thirty minutes. Being together did not always promote conversations. There were times when we just held each other's hands without saying a word—after reading the newspaper, a book, or a magazine or while watching the opera or symphony channels on television. Silence was golden, and the feeling of peace descended on Anita before she retired to sleep.

Scoreboard

Anita: 13; Alzheimer's: 8

My dearest diary, these were productive listening times, and I continued to learn from my mentor. I learned how to enjoy various forms of music and operas, and I gained patience to wait for her responses. I learned about achieving peace of mind and needed to learn to forgive and accept my circumstances. She taught me that it was okay to say, "I love you." I could say it to other people in a silent way, including complete strangers. The box of life's protection was breaking down little by little as we visited together.

Scoreboard

Anita: 14; Alzheimer's: 8

It is okay to open up yourself to someone after you learn to trust that person. It was good to hold hands and allow love to enter into our hearts. Yes, this amazing lady who had Alzheimer's was my mentor. She never stopped teaching this student.

One evening in early February, I arrived at the center really late. The attendee informed me that Anita did not want to go to bed until she saw me. She scolded me because I was the one holding up Anita's bedtime. *What?* That is when I made sure that I arrived by seven. It gave Anita time to enjoy the wheelchair outings. This was important to Anita.

It flashed in my memory what one of the family's caregivers had mentioned. When the staff moved Tom out of their bedroom to another room to sleep in his own hospital bed, Anita's heart almost gave up. It tore them apart. She was so distraught because her husband could no longer sleep with her. Each evening before bed, she would kiss him, and they would hold each other for a very long time as she bent over his hospital bed. At night he would call out to her, and she would hear his voice and go to him. Getting old is okay. Turning elderly must be miserable. Someone else takes over the responsibilities of an elderly person's life.

Anita and I appeared to have so much in common. It seemed like we had known each other all of our lives, but where? Where did she remember me? Where did we meet that I couldn't remember her?

Somehow she knew I needed to step out of my protective box. On the other hand, I did not know I needed to allow myself to open up to receive her love. My protective safety walls prevented anyone from reaching out to me, including Anita. To allow giving love to others was easy. However, to open my heart up to *receive* something for myself was extremely hard because it was just plain hard to receive things. As for Anita, this special lady reached out to me, and in return, she needed my love. What was Anita trying to convey to me?

One evening when I was visiting Anita, I noticed her hands had veins located just under the thin skin where there were no muscles, yet those hands were still strong. Her heartbeat kept traveling through to mine as if pumping electrical currents. We looked into each other's eyes and accepted challenges to walk again. The opportunity for Anita to regain independence ignited her hope. Anita *did* indeed learn to follow directions and walked again, but how long would her freedom last? When would the next disappointment arrive?

Scoreboard

Anita: 15; Alzheimer's: 8

I asked myself why Lynn had issues with her mother, but I knew it was none of my business. She never came with me to see her mother at the center. Perhaps it was for the best. Lynn's heart would have been crushed to see her mother respond to me with enthusiasm. So I learned to accept this plight in life.

During one evening visit, the staff offered us a private room. I said, "Sure." I remembered its location because the room's door was open the first time I had entered the center.

As I was pushing Anita's wheelchair down the long hallway, she started to move the wheelchair with her legs. The wheelchair moved faster and faster. Those skinny legs had strong muscles. I could barely keep up with this determined woman.

Then suddenly, the wheelchair slowed down. We came to the short hallway that led to the front door. Anita knew exactly where that front door was located. She motioned for me to push her wheelchair toward it. Together, we moved closer and closer. Opened or closed, a person could clearly see cars parked outside. I stopped the wheelchair to open the visitors' room.

It was nighttime, and the sliding glass door would not open automatically. Anita must have felt tricked. Would she forget that I had taken her so close to the front door? It would be extremely disappointing if that front door had automatically opened but she had not been allowed to go through it. On the other hand, there would have been a huge smile on her devious face as she accomplished an escape.

As I peered into Anita's face, I saw her eyes looking straight ahead at that double door. She did want to escape. How often had she challenged herself to remember where this escape route was located?

Sadly, Anita appeared stunned when I pointed the wheelchair toward the visitors' room. She just kept turning her head, looking at the front door. I pulled the wheelchair into the small room and then closed the door. Anita kept looking at that closed door, and then she reached to open it. I explained how if I took her out that front door, I would need to take her home. She looked at me with a warm smile.

"It would be wonderful to grant you this wish, but then everyone would be searching for us, including the police. We would be caught," I tried to explain to her.

I carefully continued to explain that she would be returned to the center, and I would no longer be allowed to visit. Her deep desire to return to her beloved husband and love seat would continue unfilled. I did not have the authority to take Anita out that front door. Somehow Anita comprehended what I was saying. Both of our hearts sank.

Scoreboard

Anita: 15; Alzheimer's: 9

For a person who had Alzheimer's, Anita's brain sometimes connected our silent conversations. This often baffled me. Alzheimer's blackens out different parts of the brain, but somehow she had not totally lost her comprehension.

After sitting a very short time in the small room, the door opened. Anita did not look toward the center's front door this time, but I did. I would have loved to take Anita through that front door and back to Tom. Unfortunately, I could not turn back time.

Part 3

The next day I joined Anita for lunch. Her food had not arrived at her table. I could tell she was getting anxious to eat. She kept grabbing on to the tablecloth. I asked myself, "How should I handle this possibly upsetting situation?" I thought quickly.

"Anita, would you like to go to a restaurant or a cafe?" I whispered.

She responded, "Doughnut." This just surprised everyone around the table because no one had ever heard Anita speak. I asked Anita to close her eyes and pretend she was walking on a city street somewhere in Sweden. She could stop and smell all the wonderful pastries. The other table partners were smiling, perhaps joining us on that stroll in their thoughts.

Anita began showing that family smile. As we pretended to enter a pastry shop, her lunch food arrived. I told Anita to pretend the center's food was the best doughnut she had ever eaten. That day Anita ate most of her food.

Scoreboard

Anita: 16; Alzheimer's: 9

Another day about a week later during lunchtime, I arrived very late. I pulled up a chair beside Anita's table. The attendant questioned my presence. I informed her that I watched over Anita and asked if she had a problem with that. Then it happened again. Anita didn't want to eat.

The attendant instantly reached over me to Anita and firmly squeezed Anita's cheeks to force her to open her mouth. After that, she took a tablespoon full of food, shoveled the food into Anita's slightly opened mouth, and then covered Anita's mouth with her fingers so that Anita could not spit the food out. I was so shocked by the way that my mentor was being mistreated. That instantly infuriated me.

The food became lodged in Anita's throat. I encouraged Anita to open her mouth and spit some of the food out. There was no response. I tried to encourage her to open her month just a little and sip a spoonful of water. There was no response. I thought the water might dislodge the food and help slide it down her throat, but it didn't. I needed to think faster.

She kept gagging and gagging and gagging. She was turning slightly purple. Action! I took my hands and gently vibrated her throat. It took many tries, but it worked. Eventually, all of that crushed food turned slushy because it finally drained down into her stomach. Anita's coloring returned, and I started to relax. Well, a little. It was so hard for me to hold back my anger and tears. When I looked at the attendant, she looked at me with uncaring eyes and coldly commented, "Anita does not like to eat, so she is forced to eat."

Scoreboard

Anita: 16; Alzheimer's: 10

As I was pushing Anita's wheelchair away from the lunch table, the attendant mentioned something that again stunned me. She briefly mentioned that the food from each plate is weighed so that they can see how much each patient eats. I remembered my mother's food was checked and weighed too. Maybe the lunch attendant could have been a little gentler with Anita. After all, each patient has the right to dignity.

Scoreboard

Anita: 16; Alzheimer's: 11

I never told Lynn about this particular experience.

A very funny incident happened on a different afternoon. I had been to the salon to have a perm. My dearest diary, when I stopped to visit Anita, she screamed really loud for help and said, "Some stranger has come to wheel me away." She was totally petrified. She did not recognize me at all.

Scoreboard

Anita: 16; Alzheimer's: 12

A nurse quickly came to her rescue. She looked into Anita's eyes and let her know that JJ was there. Immediately, Anita calmed down. I continued to push her wheelchair over by the water fountain, dribbled water on the pink sponge, and encouraged Anita to drink from the sponge. Quizzically, she looked at me. I quietly stated, "I'm JJ." I explained I had had my hair curled and promised never to do i again. I have kept that promise to this day.

Scoreboard

Anita: 17; Alzheimer's: 12

During most early-evening hours, Anita was sitting in her wheelchair, usually waiting for me in the hallway close to her room. I would inquire if she would like to have some water, view some pictures, go to bed, listen to me read to her, watch some TV, and/or have her hair combed. Now Anita replied by reaching out toward the fountain instead of saying yes. I needed to be very careful as she sipped the water because it could drain into her lungs and cause pneumonia.

Next, we usually took a nature stroll, looking at various paintings hanging on the walls. Simple phrases like "blue lake" or "clouds in the sky" were often part of our conversations. Some pictures had "green hills" or "high mountains" with "snow." It made me feel like I was talking down to this highly intelligent lady. I couldn't tell if she remembered viewing the many nature pictures or just enjoyed the art, or perhaps she literally forgot the outings.

Sometimes after slowly strolling around, I would ask Anita if she would like to stop to see the fireplace. Over time we spent many hours in front of it. She appeared to be soothed each time she watched the fire.

Anita's family home had two fireplaces. I suspect sitting by the center's fireplace and viewing it brought back a few memories as she shut her eyes. I would like to think she was pretending that she had returned home and that she was sitting across from her special man on her love seat by the large bay window near their warm, glowing fireplace. It was a peaceful time for Anita just before she was prepared for her evening sleep.

Scoreboard

Anita: 18; Alzheimer's: 12

One very warm late-winter afternoon, I had a big surprise. I asked Anita if she would like to go outside and sit in the center's live garden area for a few minutes. We could place a blanket over her lap and legs. She could enjoy some fresh air on that warm winter afternoon with the sun shining on real plants. Anita replied, "No." She loved nature, but she knew the difference after touching the various fake indoor plants with stems and leaves only once. Anita knew what she wanted, and I was not going to intrude with more questions. I never asked her about going outside again.

During another warm sunny afternoon, Anita was pretty spunky. She was learning to walk again and felt very confident. She wanted us to go for a short walk. We never went on walks. We went on wheelchair outings. On this particular afternoon while watching an opera on TV, I noticed Anita's attention was pointed to the ceiling.

"Anita, what do you see?" I inquired as she continued looking at the ceiling. "Where would you like to travel?" She still didn't give an answer.

Then a few minutes later, she said, "See our cabin." Anita briefly mentioned the family cabin by the private lake. I asked her if she could see any animals. "Some deer. Fish with Tom," she muttered. "Once a black bear," she said with a partial smile. This was one of those great days when Anita spoke very slowly in just a few words.

Scoreboard

Anita: 19; Alzheimer's: 12

Part 4

That night a light snow covered parts of the ground, alerting everyone that spring was not arriving early. It melted during the day, but temperatures dropped the next night, leaving icy main roads in the mornings and black-ice patches on side streets until early afternoons. I promised Lynn I would see her mother at least in the daytime and then report back.

Those cold winter days made my knuckles turn white with fear, gripping the steering wheel after seeing shiny spots on the road. I was so scared of the slippery ice. Yet even the fear of driving didn't overpower Lynn's only opportunity to hear how her mother's day had gone. Lynn needed peace of mind, and her need was far more important than my fear of driving on the icy side streets.

Lynn's emails sounded like she was exhausted balancing her roles as daughter to aging parents, wife to a loving husband, and worker. Taking care of her parents took up so much of her time. She needed to escape.

My attention often switched to Lynn's health concerns even more than Anita's.

Message dated 2/18/07 11:18 AM (Partial email)

My Stranger Friend, it sounds like to me you need a valium… that is not a "slam" to you, those days are long gone. I misjudged you and I admit it… It still sounds like you need a valium. I'm taking the weekend "off" from my mother. She's in good hands and I NEED A BREAK… this is all too much for me. It's just too much… so for this weekend IT'S ALL ABOUT ME! I'm going to enjoy life, and be happy… I'm in my "fabulous sixties" and nobody is going to take this away from Me! … remember to laugh! Lynn

I thought back to the previous month when I gave Lynn a teddy bear, hoping it might help comfort her and bring down the stress level. It was a leftover teddy bear donation from First Book, an organization that Senator Murray started years ago to help children receive a start-up home library. I was very proud of this accomplishment because it helped children want to learn to read. My only book growing up besides the Bible was a children's book about Frederick Douglass. I loved that simple book. There must be other children who would love to have more than one book to call their own and enjoy reading in their homes. That's why First Book was so important to me, not to mention I got to hand out cuddly teddy bears.

When I handed Lynn the teddy bear, she looked at it and laughed, commenting that she used to make fun of people who had toy animals, especially teddy bears. I thought back to her tears. Now she appeared to just want to escape from life's circumstances. I didn't blame her. I remembered what Lynn had written in her emails. At least the teddy bear worked for a little while.

Message dated 1/16/07 9:41 AM (Partial email)

...driving home I clung onto that brown teddy bear. My tears drenched the bear's head. Thank you. Lynn

Message dated 1/20/07 10:18 AM (Partial email)

... I took my bear down to the local embroidery place, it's a "she bear." For ten bucks they made me a little t-shirt for her. On the front it says, "MOM." She now rides with me everywhere in car's back seat. So, so silly, but can you believe the comfort that bear has given this 61-year-old woman. A simple teddy bear allows me something to hang on to. Anyway, she's got a permanent "ride" in my car. Thanks again... Lynn

"Remember me" escalated to describing Lynn to a tee because even she realized her stress level and the importance of being remembered. Perhaps everyone wants to be remembered in some way. Maybe that's why some people drink. Lynn was starting to notice that her life had a purpose. Now she wanted to become more involved as a wife.

Lynn was already thinking of ways to show her hubby how special he was to her. It was a huge step for this woman who normally was whimsical and loved surprises.

Later I surprised Lynn with a blanket from Wrap Them with Love, a homemade quilt business where quilting bees can send their homemade quilts. The founder will locate needy and hurting people who can use these lovingly made quilts, which are sent all around the world. What a wonderful business helping to comfort people around the world. I really meant to forward three quilts to some children; however, in Lynn's case, she was hurting really badly. I had a small throw quilt that had pictures of horses, and I remembered Lynn telling me how she deeply loved horses and hoped that someday she would have her own horse. Her mother thought Lynn was just going through some emotions, but Lynn was honest with herself and knew the importance of owning a horse.

Lynn's eyes became so big when she saw the *gift*. She even asked if it was really for her. Of course, I asked her if she would like a larger quilt for herself and one for her hubby. My heart warmed as I gazed upon the horse quilt draped over a love seat at her home after Lynn passed away. I asked her hubby if I could have it; however, he said he would like to keep it. How special of him. What a wonderful memory. That's what Wrap Them in Love is all about.

Meanwhile, that Sunday, seeing Lynn's health condition reminded me to eat more balanced foods and drink more water. The stresses in life must be controlled during various seasons. Meeting other people can be stressful, but crossing paths is still so important.

My dearest diary, I've read that eating good food, drinking good water, and exercising the mind and body can slow down and prevent Alzheimer's in people. Lynn and her mother prepared and ate good foods and drank loads of water. According to Lynn, they drank water all the time plus some beer and wine now and then. Neither Lynn nor her mother wanted to gain any weight or look heavy like me, so they felt that health was very important.

Lynn said she liked salads. I wondered if Lynn drank smoothies because Lynn's body needed more than salads. She enjoyed eating when she was hungry; however, smoking kept the hunger away most of the time. Because of the stress Lynn was going through, the doctor prescribed a drug that checked her emotions. The drug also affected

Lynn's eating habits. She didn't want to eat very much. After one of our personal conversations regarding meat being a good protein, a few nights later Lynn informed me that she and her hubby enjoyed a great steak. A juicy steak is one of my favorite foods.

Lynn just appeared to be very knowledgeable about good eating habits, but why was she losing so much weight? My mind raced for answers, and absolutely none appeared until Lynn mentioned again that she took some drug that cut down her desire to eat. What kind of drug would do that to a person's body?

Her food world was so different than mine. I loved a plate with a small steak, potatoes, vegetables, and salad followed by a bowl of vanilla ice cream with hot fudge. I couldn't relate to what she was talking about or writing in her emails. She would eat only a simple salad. Returning my thoughts to good eating habits, I finally stepped forward and asked if she liked smoothies. Some health magazines mentioned that smoothies were healthy for the on-the-go person who didn't have time for a fully balanced meal. I commented that smoothies tasted good and energized my body. The smoothies were full of vitamins and minerals. Of course, salads were healthy, but Lynn kept losing weight.

I told Lynn about *The Everything Alzheimer's Book*. Page 172 under "Lunch Recipes," there was a wonderful smoothie recipe. It's really so simple.

Smoothie Recipe

Take a half cup of apple juice or orange juice and a half cup of water,
1 banana,
A half cup of frozen blueberries,
3 tablespoons of protein power.
Then blend together.

This was so simple that even a person who, like me, wasn't good in the kitchen could easily make this smoothie. Throughout the years looking through various cooking magazines, I've located other recipes for smoothies. They are great energy builders, and they don't have that chalky taste.

Comparing the three of us, Anita was a fabulous cook. Hiring a cook would be Lynn's and my dream come true. Lynn and I laughed, conversing about how our husbands could utilize the kitchen. Her hubby cooked most of the time. He could cook anything. Mine could grill fabulous steaks. To this day, he whips up breakfast every morning for me.

I told Lynn that my sister could walk into a kitchen and that all the cupboard doors would fly open. I could just hear every pot, pan, and dish; containers of all sorts; and even the stove and oven calling out and competing to be what she would use next in the kitchen—"No, use me!"

To this day, if I walk into the kitchen or even close to the vicinity, I find every cupboard door is tightly closed and there's no noise. Even the microwave door squeaks when I open it. Forget the oven. Oh, I told Lynn I could only bake one of those wonderful premade pies.

Many times that wonderful sound of Lynn's laughter filled the air. She didn't like cooking either. Thank God Almighty for sending us wonderful husbands.

Then I mentioned to Lynn that I was worried about *food* for my mother, who had decided to come stay for the weekend. I asked a friend if she would show me how to cook something simple that was healthy. She provided some homemade stew that tasted delicious. My mom commented on how great the stew tasted. She never knew it was from a friend. I didn't lie to my mother. I just didn't confess it was a friend who made the stew. Lynn sure did laugh.

I explained to Lynn that on that Saturday morning when my mom stayed overnight, we enjoyed breakfast—eggs, toast, bacon, and smoothies. Our bodies would be filled with lasting energy to start our busy day.

Lynn only remained quiet on rare occasions. Had she drank smoothies before? Lynn didn't respond to this subject. As a woman who wasn't good in the kitchen, she must have known about simple health drinks like these.

Several years later I located a fantastic energy product filled with loads of natural minerals and vitamins. It is high in protein, low in fat, and smart about calories, and it also utilizes the benefits of prebiotics. Several times a week I create an energy smoothie filled with fresh or frozen fruit as well as natural minerals and vitamins. My simple foods have advanced to tasty smoothies that I can share with family, friends, and guests.

These two entwined ladies would be very proud of me, and I'm proud of myself too. Following their earlier example in life to eat healthier foods has helped me make better meal choices. I even eat more salads now.

For years I had been striving to lose some weight, but those fatty areas loved claiming their territory. They didn't like intruders like diets. But the fat breaks down with salads and drinks. Then it laughs and multiplies more. I found another way to help eliminate some of that fat around my middle. I lost forty-three pounds, and today I laugh because I've beaten the weight gain. It took me a good year, but none of those fat cells have returned to their treasured meeting places. Every person's body is unique. However, for me I can now jog a short distance. Perhaps Lynn would be surprised to learn that I can do two push-ups. Again, these two entwined ladies would be so very proud of me, and I'm proud of myself too.

Part 5

My mind returned to Anita. She was fighting pneumonia again. As for Lynn, she was constantly overloaded with these realities.

When this devoted daughter traveled to the family home during the week, her papa would decide whether to visit his wife. Tom missed his wife so much, but her screaming, "Get out!" was breaking everyone's hearts. Lynn confirmed again to me how she noticed the family home was peaceful without her mother's presence.

Scoreboard

Anita: 19; Alzheimer's: 13

About two weeks before Anita's birthday, I asked her what she would like as a present. During this time she was suffering with a bout of pneumonia. "To go dancing," responded Anita. I asked her if she would like to close her eyes and remember the times when Tom held her tight in his arms and danced to slow music. I would be willing to gently push her wheelchair around the receptionist's open space as if she pretended to dance with her beloved hubby. "No," she carefully said. This day her mind was 100 percent great.

Scoreboard

Anita: 20; Alzheimer's: 13

Part 6

What determination this spunky person had. A little more than a month earlier, she'd decided to start walking, and she succeeded. Her goal was to return home. Maybe then her hubby could take her in his shaky arms and they could gently have one last time dancing together since her hip had completely healed. Of course, there would need two adults to help them dance—each adult holding on to this elderly couple so that no one would fall. Or perhaps this dancing could happen at the center? At least it was a lovely thought.

Several days later in the afternoon while trying to get out of bed, she fell, hit her head, split her scalp open, and cracked her other hip. This frail lady just could not win.

Scoreboard

Anita: 20; Alzheimer's: 14

When I arrived at the center, her bed was empty. My heart dropped, sinking to the floor. I checked my phone. There were no phone calls from Lynn. That was a good sign. I checked with the center's front desk, and they informed me that she had been taken to the local hospital's emergency room a couple of hours earlier. Immediately, I alerted the center that I was driving over to the hospital to see whether it would be okay to stay and keep Anita company.

Upon arrival, I alerted the front desk receptionist that I was not family and explained that I was Anita's daughter's friend who checked up on her mother every day. I also wanted to inquire about how Anita was doing. I requested permission to be with this Alzheimer's patient. The employee at the front desk gave me a very nice smile. She wrote something down on a file and led me to Anita's location. Maybe the center's nursing station had phoned the emergency room and alerted them it was okay for me to stay with Anita until Lynn arrived. If so, then they have my thanks.

Anita was on a hospital bed in the hallway, waiting for a doctor to check her for a skull fracture. Blood was still fresh in her hair. Anita sure did know how to bang up her head. The cut was deep and needed stitches. I asked Anita if she knew she was in the emergency room. Amazingly, without saying one word, she reached up and touched the open spot. I asked her not to touch it, and she immediately pulled back her hand. Wow! She understood what I was communicating to her. I constantly talked and talked and talked to Anita. I knew that if she had a concussion, it would not be good for her to sleep. Anita's eyes were not open, but she informed me she heard every word. She was listening to everything I was saying.

Scoreboard

Anita: 21; Alzheimer's: 15 (both won)

I phoned Lynn, and I informed her about the circumstance. I asked her if she was on the way. I also asked her if she would like to say something to her mother. Lynn snapped, "My mother cannot understand me." I put the phone next to Anita's ear. I asked Anita who she was. This fabulous lady became irritated. "My name is Anita. *A-N-I-T-A*. Now shut up!"

"Who was that?" Lynn asked. I told her it was her mother speaking. "My mother has Alzheimer's and can no longer speak," she said in total denial.

I tried to be gentle in my approach. "Yes, Lynn, there are times when your mother can't speak, but sometimes she still can. Most of the time she mumbles. Today she is speaking clearly. Your mother fell and cut her head. When can you arrive at the emergency room? She needs stitches, and I'm not family."

There was silence at the other end. After a few moments, Lynn said she would drive to the emergency room as soon as possible. It would take her an hour and a half, depending upon traffic. I thanked her.

There must have been something in Anita's file that granted me permission to stay with her during these trying moments. Not only was I allowed to keep her company while waiting in the hallway, but I was asked to accompany her when they checked her for a concussion. I made sure to tell every medical person that I was not a relative but rather Anita's friend.

Several hours later as the nurse was preparing Anita for the doctor, she took a needle filled with Novocain and stuck it into the deep cut in order to numb the area for stitches. "Why are you hurting me?" Anita questioned as if she was a small child who had fallen, and someone had placed some iodine on a scratch. Luckily, Lynn arrived just as the doctor was about to give Anita stitches. What a relief.

After this experience my relationship with Anita grew even deeper. Then one noontime when I was going between workplaces on a sunny day, I dashed to the center. Lynn was there with her husband. What a very nice-looking couple.

Lynn introduced us, and then I turned my attention toward Anita. She looked so peaceful. I lifted the sheet that covered her hands to check if her fingernails were clean. Next, I checked her hair and teeth, and then I gave her a gentle kiss on the forehead. Lynn wanted to say something to me, but her hubby motioned for her to watch what I was doing. I would not change what I normally did in front of any medical or center employees, and I wouldn't change that in front of Lynn and her husband either.

On our way out, Lynn casually commented about her mother asking where her other daughter was. I brushed this comment off because I assumed Anita must have been talking about a friend or another relative. During our Sunday conversation, Lynn brought up the subject again. It was strange for Lynn to comment that she thought her mom was talking about me.

The following day I brought up the subject of the "other daughter" to Anita. Her head turned toward my face, and she gave me that family smile through her glassy eyes. She reached her hand out to mine. I smiled and slightly giggled. I looked into her eyes and said with a joke, "Does that mean you want to be my other mother?" Her eyes lit up and grasped my hand firmly. I really was important to this lovely author besides just someone who had her books. This common stranger was outside her comfort zone, and I still wanted to chuckle to myself.

Then it happened. Anita looked directly in my eyes just like the first time we met. She saw right down into my soul. At that moment something happened. I gazed back into Anita's eyes, and I said with my eyes, "If I ever would have wanted another mother, it would be you." Anita's eyes became glassy as we continued to stare into each other's hearts. What a very personal moment in time. Where did we meet?

Our paths must have really met through her prayers because I couldn't figure out where we had seen or meet before. It could have been at a thrift store or food market since we lived a couple of miles apart. Was it Tom and her walking down the circular staircase at the opera house when I attended one opera some forty years earlier? I shrugged my shoulders and dismissed the idea.

Anita knew how to break down my safeguards and get me out of the box I liked living in for security. I loved my own mother, so why would I have a hidden desire for another mother? I knew that my mother didn't encourage me to be a police officer or work in the medical field when I mentioned this to her as a teenager. She even dismissed the idea of me receiving a degree in the field of education. She did encourage me to attend college. After college my parents thought I would return home and locate work at a processing or manufacturing plant. On the other hand, Anita looked at me as if I had writing talents. What did my subconscious tell Anita compared to my own mother? I didn't like to learn that my safety zone was being invaded. Why had I allowed this very special person into *my* personal life?

Scoreboard

Anita: 22; Alzheimer's: 15

It was amazing how easy it had been to fulfill my promise not to forget this very special lady who had asked me into her life. It was so impressive the way she could still use her left and right brain during this late stage of Alzheimer's. I hoped she would never realize my IQ was not even close to hers.

I never discussed the time I hit my head on our wooden couch when I was diving after my cat. I hit my head so hard that it must have caused a concussion. I had a headache for days. I used to be an excellent speller, and I could remember names, dates, and events. Since hitting my head so hard on that wood frame there are many times that I don't always remember people's names or dates, but I can remember events. I've heard hitting our heads can cause brain issues at a later date. I wondered if this is what happened to Anita. Did she hit her head once, and did that eventually cause Alzheimer's to start at a later date? Besides hitting her head could not forgiving someone or something be part of Alzheimer's?

Within two months, Lynn's emails reeked of jealousy, and there was much envy between us three ladies. She longed to hear the words "I love you" from her mother. Lynn wanted me to be around her mother, but I was always supposed to remember that Anita was her mother, not mine. This mother's question about her "other daughter" was messing up the good relationship that had been developing between Lynn and me. I never said anything to Lynn. She just knew. I never looked at Anita as my mother until she called me the "other daughter" and tightly held my hand. From that moment on, she became even more special to my heart. Something popped in my subconscious. Somehow Anita's partial smile triggered a silent response. Lynn needed to understand that her mother was my mentor; not my mother.

This family would not appreciate my interfering. I know I would not appreciate someone doing that with *my* family. Somehow there was something building even stronger between Anita and me. Periodically, she would look directly in my eyes and down to my soul. What a gifted person! She sure did know people's hearts.

Anita needed to say to Lynn from her own lips, "I love you." These were very precious words, and to hear them from her mother's lips might cover the deep hurts from the past inside her. Hopefully, it would trigger forgiveness, and the beginning of envy would subside.

With forgiveness, a person is able to forget and move forward. The devil loves to attack and attack and attack with old memories. Those demons just will not leave. As for me, I usually call the demon by name (the demon of jealousy, for example) and inform that demon that it must leave and never return in the Name of Jesus. Then I command that demon—again in the Name of Jesus—to go to the deepest part of the ocean and enter into a fishlike creature. The demon is to remain there until Jesus releases it to hell. Speaking with authority in the Name of Jesus over the situation is vital. Yet there are times when speaking means nothing because I am still holding on to hurts or wrong attitudes. Does non-forgiveness delay the power of authority? I've learned it sure does.

Could this mother and daughter last long enough to forgive each other? I know sometimes I have not been able to fully forgive myself or others, and it has stopped me from moving forward. I need to confess what is weighing down my heart. Confessing by speaking Jesus's blood to cover my unworthiness relieves these deep hurts. There have been times when I have informed God the Father that I just cannot forgive and forget. He will need to do it for me or at least help me rely on the cross. With forgiveness, I don't even remember any problems, differences, or issues.

I wanted to ask Anita about her faith and how she was able to handle hard times, but time had taken so much from her ability to communicate. I wondered how at times she could stand tall with her head up. I remembered how deeply hard it was to forgive myself and my hubby when we lost our home and had to declare bankruptcy because of the economy. It was more than depressing. It drained so much energy and confidence to make life-changing decisions for months. I wanted someone to hold my hand and tell me what all the legal paperwork and directions meant. There was one gal who had compassion and was there for me. OR There was one gal who was compassionate and was there for me. I wondered if Anita or Lynn had ever gone through this type of mess in their lives. During a Sunday conversation, Lynn brought me an investment book. It included how to make out a will. Sadly, Lynn didn't create a living will, but my hubby and I had done so years earlier.

During this time period, my mind would be foggy one day while a different day it was okay, but my self-confidence was not the same. I loved those totally clear days. Some days were filled with hopelessness, and I would lose the feeling that I was a worthy human being with talents, skills, and experiences. Days turned into weeks, and months turned into a couple of years. I could not function correctly on a daily basis. Actually, it was moment-by-moment survival. Thinking and making any type of decision was so hard. It caused my constant depression and negative attitudes, but that was not a good way to live. One observation from my mentor was there is a positive future. Anita's words kept lingering in my mind. *Shoulders back, head up. Stop sniffling. Move forward!* Smiling, I agreed that good times were on their way, and I would think positively. Well, most of the time.

Was this what Lynn went through on a continual basis with her bipolar disorder? My trial by fire was really filled with stinky smoke. There were no sweet roses to smell in any way. I kept remembering that we were not the only family going through this dreadful economic time period. There wasn't any more time for a pity party.

Life becomes difficult, but with love, life isn't totally unbearable. The economic times were so very sad for so many people. Anita had her own business writing books. She didn't need employees and could work whenever she wanted. She was very lucky. Lynn always worked for someone else, so she couldn't understand. And I wasn't about to tell her about my circumstances.

I don't think I have forgiven myself for making extremely bad decisions in the past and being a bad wife at times. How I wanted to be a good wife and honor my hubby. I failed because I would not firmly stand up for what was right. We lost everything. There was no use crying and feeling sorry for myself. I must remember my mentor encouraging me to see a future with hope.

Sometimes even a death gives hope for a positive future. It surprised me that I had very few tears when my parents went to their eternal home. But the flowing waterfalls for Anita's passing opened up a desire for more out of life. It was like my mind heard Anita reprimand me again and again. *Shoulders back, head up. Stop sniffling! Move forward!* What a positive way of encouragement.

Looking back, I realize that the three of us loved animals. When we had to give up our home, it was hard seeing my two wild cats sitting on our front steps. It had been six weeks since moving out of our forty year-old home. Driving by to check up on how the lawn looked, I saw my precious two cats waiting for food. I broke down then and there. For years I made sure they received fresh water and food by our front doorstep no matter what season. They had not forgotten me. These two trusting little creatures must have thought I had abandoned them, and I was forced to do so. I tried to touch them like before, but the one had turned into wild eyes and didn't seem to recognize me. The other allowed me to pet him. His name was Silver. I explained what happened, and Silver appeared to understand. The other cat sat at a distance and listened too. It's the one time I broke down, and I wept right in front of those two wild cats. Who would take time to care for these wild creatures? Two wonderful neighbors, Denise and Cheryl, reached out and started feeding these dear ones. Thank you!

JJ Janice

Looking back, I realize that home was part of my safe zone. Anita was in her comfort zone when she was typing in her small homemade room in her basement. As for Lynn, I don't know where her safety area was located.

Chapter 11

Facing Reality

During the morning hours in the second week of April, Anita soared to heaven. Not one family member was present. Only the angels held Anita's hands and escorted her to the peaceful eternal sphere. That afternoon around four o'clock, Lynn contacted me about Anita's passing.

Lynn did not sound distressed. There was a relief in her voice because her mother did not hurt any longer. Alzheimer's lost the pleasure of totally taking her mother's memories. Instead Anita beat that disease. Or did she?

Scoreboard

Anita won. Alzheimer's won. (Both were winners.)

Anita gave her beautiful daughter, Lynn, the best gift of love. Two days before she passed, Anita clearly said, "I love you." It was one gift that came from the deepest part of her mother's heart to her daughter, Lynn. Anita's three words uplifted her loving little girl, who was now a fulfilled woman.

Lynn accepted responsibilities, knowing she was a good daughter, smiling with the realization that she had completed her faithful duties to one of her parents. Now it was still time to care for her father. She had seen loneliness in their family home. Her parents had been married for so long, and they enjoyed seeing one another, talking together, and being together each day. This separation was gnawing away at Tom and Lynn as they realized the huge void in life now. Just because someone passes away doesn't mean he or she is instantly forgotten.

This observant daughter desperately wanted to step forward in her mother's leadership. Would the family allow her to be the new matriarch? It would be up to Lynn to contact everyone her parents knew and inform them about her mother's passing. It would be up to her to work with the family to take care of the private cremation services.

Lynn would still care for her beloved papa. His health issues were very serious as a result of his three heart attacks. She was not sure how much longer he could survive. It was very hard on Tom the last several months without his beloved wife by his side. He continued shouting his wife's name at night. Anita's last words to him were, "Get out!" according to Lynn. What a crushing last encounter.

The day after Anita left this earth's world, Lynn phoned and requested that I drive to her parents' home. Once again, Tom looked out the big bay window and waved to me. A tall, slender figure walked past Tom to the front door. I pulled my emotions together, slowly taking one step at a time. Lynn pushed that front door wide open and welcomed me with that family smile. Our hug was extremely firm and long. I guessed we both needed that moment of time. I started to inwardly laugh as we hugged because I could feel Lynn's back muscles. They were so firm compared to her mother's back muscles.

Tom received my condolences. It was good to know that he approved of my entering his home with his devoted daughter. Tom's greeting and warm smile let me know that I was still accepted and maybe still useful during this stressful time. A friend came over, and everyone talked. She only stayed for a very short time, and she brought some goodies for the family. When she left, she looked at me, "Who are you? I don't remember Anita mentioning anything about you."

I simply replied, "We've known each other a lifetime." The lady looked puzzled and walked to her car.

Lynn motioned for me to follow her. We walked down a short hallway to the back bedrooms. I mentioned that her parents' picture looked fabulous. Lynn said she had taken the picture. Wow! What a great photographer. Then she stopped walking and turned her head toward me. "My mother did not show you the pictures on this wall?"

I replied, "No, we sat in the living room and talked about books, education, students, cultures, and places to travel."

The look on her face was really like a big surprise gift. She was totally caught off guard that her mother had not shown me the family pictures and the various rooms in their home. Why would Anita have done that? As we entered her mother's bedroom, Lynn explained there was a need for her father to have his own special bed because of his health. Lynn inquired, "Didn't my mother show you her bedroom?"

"No. Why would she?" I again repeated how we always stayed in the living room and mentioned a few times I had said hello to her father in the TV room.

Walking into Anita's bedroom was really personal to me. I felt very uncomfortable because it belonged to the family. Lynn picked up one of her mother's favorite silver sweaters and smelled it. "It smells like my mother," she said. Then she handed it to me. I smelled it, and she was right. It did have that soft sweet fragrance of a clean elderly woman. Anita had worn that sweater for her birthday a year earlier I wanted to clinch it in my arms and hold it close to my chest, but I didn't.

There was a camera on the bed along with a dried pink rose I had given to Anita for her birthday a couple of weeks earlier. There were other items I can no longer picture in my mind. Lynn spoke with hardly a voice, explaining how she couldn't sleep in her mother's bed, even though she was extremely tired and needed a good night's sleep. Then she mentioned she needed help in choosing some clothes for her mother's cremation service. We agreed upon the silver sweater.

Anita looked so beautiful in it with her white hair. Sadly, it turned out no clothes were needed for the cremation event.

Every inch of Anita's room was filled to the brim. You could barely see the walls near the ceiling. The bed was located under the window, and the bright afternoon light shined on each item on the bed. To the left of the bed was an old vanity with a medium-sized, rectangular mirror, a dresser, and bookshelves. More shelves filled with papers and clothes filled the other side of the room. The room smelled like roses, but there was only the one dried-up rose. My mind raced, wondering how often these items had traveled around the world and finally moved into this modest family home more than forty-five years earlier.

We returned to the living room and talked with each other. Actually, it was really Lynn who constantly talked and talked and talked to her papa and me. Lynn was a great talker, and sometimes I was not sure what to believe and what not to believe. She mentioned that a good con artist is one who can say anything and have the listener believe it. Was Lynn trying to convince me that she was a con artist? What a funny subject to bring up after losing her mother.

It was Lynn's birthday on April 21. She was glad that her mom had not died on her birthday. Then I brought up the subject of her mother's wedding ring. I had located Anita's wedding ring three days earlier before her death. Immediately, I phoned Lynn from Anita's room at the center, informing Lynn that I had located it. I took the ring to have it cleaned and kept that ring on my pinky finger to make sure we would not lose it again. It was a very simple thin ring with a row of small diamonds. I was so relieved to take that ring off my finger and safely placed it in Lynn's palm. That was another promise I was able to keep for Lynn.

Lynn went to her papa, knelt in front of him, and showed him her mother's wedding ring. As he gazed upon it, she requested that she keep the ring in remembrance of her mother. Her caring father's eyes filled with tears, and as the father and daughter gazed upon each other's faces, he replied, "Yes, it is yours." I almost lost it. My eyes filled with tears too. Some moments should be far more private.

I asked Lynn if she needed any help taking down, changing, or packing anything at this point. She smiled and quietly commented, "Later. Not now."

Four days later Lynn phoned, asking if I would be willing to drive her papa, her hubby, the caregiver, and her to her mother's cremation service because her vehicle only sat three people. She informed me of the time and date. I knew there would be changes, and I needed to handle them. I learned that I really didn't like changes. Once again, it was God's timing for me to support this hurting father and daughter. She told me to be at her parents' home by five thirty in the morning. I would need to remain mostly awake all night because I didn't have an alarm clock.

That emotionally challenging morning arrived, and everything outside was dark because of the sun's late arrival. Looking up and gazing inside the home, everything appeared dark. I noticed only a slight light from the kitchen. Kindly, Lynn's hubby met me in the driveway and drove the car to the family's backyard. This area was flat, so Tom could easily enter and exit the car.

Lynn greeted me at the front door. The atmosphere was extremely quiet. Entering the kitchen, the caregiver informed me that Tom did not want to go to the service. Lynn said her mother's last words to her father were, "Get out!" and he had not been to the center prior to the last two weeks. What a very sad last encounter. It broke my heart seeing this elderly man slumped in his wheelchair, looking at his feeble hands, holding a damp handkerchief, and telling his daughter and caregiver he did not want to leave his home this morning. Here was a brokenhearted man. Sometimes he looked beyond his hands down at the floor, and other times he looked outside into the dark void. The caregiver was so very precious, speaking gently to this deeply hurting husband.

Meanwhile, the sun had not arrived to light up the sky. It seemed it was taking its time. Lynn and the caregiver were encouraging Tom to get dressed, but he kept saying no through his soft, cracking voice. Those words must have been such a gruesome memory for him. I can only imagine how much it would have meant to him to have had

Anita return home. He so wanted her to return home, and she so wanted to return to him too. But they would have needed additional care, and seldom can an Alzheimer's patient receive the necessary care at home. That includes the ability to handle the emotional outbursts that are often so disturbing.

Oh, my dearest diary, what I am about to tell you really happened. It was so heartbreaking to see Tom so crushed. Allow me to tell you more.

That early-April morning, light eventually lit up the golden sky. There was a faint fragrant smell of lilies in the living room, but as I glanced around the room, I didn't see any fresh flowers. Perhaps it was Anita telling me she was alive in heaven and saying, "I love you. Thanks for being there for my family." I did not mention anything to anyone about this aroma. It is interesting how the mind will play tricks on a person's emotions.

Tom continued having an extremely hard time deciding how he could possibly attend his wife's service. I noticed he sometimes glanced toward that empty love seat.

About twenty minutes later, Tom was all dressed and sitting quietly in his wheelchair. He kept rubbing his red nose with a large white handkerchief. He looked so lost. I did not look around the room. Instead I slowly walked up to Tom, knelt beside him, and looked into his tearful red eyes. He looked like a lost little puppy.

"I don't blame you for not wanting to come today. It is a path none of us want to walk. We'll walk it together." My own soft words almost made me choke as a tear fell onto my cheek. I know he saw it because we were looking into each other's eyes. I gently brushed the liquid off my cheek. I am so glad that dam did not burst.

I felt like Anita took his hand. Smiling, I quietly spoke again, "Are you ready to walk together?"

As I got up from the squatting position, a shadowy figure sat on Anita's love seat. It was Lynn. When had she come into the room? She must have listened to what I was saying to her father. Her eyes were filled with tears. She looked like a lost little girl who needed loads of hugs. I hoped she was not jealous of me speaking with her papa. Within a few minutes, the sun started to bring the morning light, eventually totally brightening the sky. That wonderful bright sun encouraged us to move forward with our obligations.

It was Lynn who helped her papa into the front car seat and buckled him up. We drove around the home to the driveway and down the lane to the main road. It felt as if Lynn had to be in total control. Yet as I glanced through the mirror to the back seat, she still looked lost.

Once again, my mind returned to Tom. He held on to that handkerchief so tightly. Perhaps he was reviewing deep memories, choosing to look down. Now and then he would look out the car's window. Lynn decided to roll down the back window and smoke. Everyone was so quiet that I turned on my rock-and-roll music. We could hardly hear it, but it was at least a little noise. I did not know what station played the symphony. Lynn suggested taking the side roads, the way she drove her papa to see her mom.

I noticed I was going twenty miles per hour in a school zone. I chuckled to myself, driving so slowly, not even twenty-five, and school wouldn't start for two and a half hours. As we continued driving, Tom turned his face toward the side road. It was where the convalescent center was located. Tom knew exactly where he was.

His mouth started to tremble. I placed my right hand firmly on his shaky left one. He did not even move or look at me. Someone was just there for him. Suddenly, it crossed my mind that maybe Lynn or someone in the back seat noticed my hand on Tom's. I slid my firm hand free off his bony fingers at the nearby stoplight. The trip lasted a good hour and a half. The car was so quiet except for the sound of the soft music. I wasn't sure if Lynn knew the right directions because her instructions were a bit sporadic.

When we arrived at the funeral parlor, Lynn immediately took over. She wanted to make sure I had plenty of film for her camera. She said that an album of today's happenings would be a good gift for everyone. When Lynn produced it though, we were all *shocked* by the pictures she chose.

JJ Janice

We found out that Anita had written notes to herself about Lynn. Lynn found two small brown paper bags filled with notes in the family basement. The notes detailed years about her life and how her mother felt. Lynn's heart was ripped apart by what her mother had written. She wanted to burn them along with her mother. Lynn left the meeting room and placed the two small brown bags deep in the coffin. Lynn told me that she was devastated by her mother's thoughts and did not want anyone to find and read them. Those were her mother's private thoughts, and the two brown bags would be burned with her body. I thought it would be like New Year's Eve when a person writes down all their hurts on paper and then places the paper on the log to burn. The new year starts a new part of that person's life.

Just before the service, I handed Lynn's hubby a small tape recorder. I asked him to record the service and later give it to Lynn that evening. She would like hearing what everyone said about her mother when she was all alone. I figured the service would be so overwhelming that she would not remember anything. Her hubby honored my request, and I found out later she appreciated the recording.

The family was fantastic, presenting positive individual comments about their memories of Anita. Then the weirdest thing happened. Lynn told the family that she would be the one to push the button for the cremation. What!

A funeral employee pushed the gurney to the oven, opened the oven, and pushed Anita's box so hard that it slid from one end of the burner back to the other end. I thought Anita's body was going to jump out! Then the employee pushed Anita's box back into the oven, closed the door, and alerted Lynn to push the green light.

Lynn looked at my shocked face, smiled, and gave me the nod to take a picture. I obeyed. Someone almost fainted. I was so stunned, but now years later I can laugh as I review the family's mouths dropping wide open, including mine, heads shaking sideways, and our eyes bugging out from shock. I firmly believe that Lynn thrived on shocking people because she just smiled!

My dearest diary, no one should go through that emotional horror!

Next, Lynn wanted a full family picture. It would be the last family picture they would take together. After the service everyone met for a very nice luncheon at a nearby restaurant. Lynn asked me to sit at her left side and her hubby on her right side. I felt like we were bookends.

Lynn told me that she was glad that I had taken all of her mother's books. Otherwise, every book would have been thrown into the garbage or burned. Then Lynn spoke words that caught my attention. She mentioned that she had not taken any pills that morning. She wanted to make sure she felt the sorrow of her mom's passing. She wanted me to know she could handle the family's grief without any prescribed drugs.

When her food arrived Lynn looked around the table. Then she took her left arm and held it above her plate. She watched to see if anyone was planning on taking food from her. It reminded me of times when people were in jail and had to protect their food.

Tom still had not received his food, so the caregiver asked me to put some of Lynn's food on a small plate and hand it to her father. Lynn looked at me as I requested some food for her papa. She allowed me to pass a couple of pieces of fish to him. Her pupils were enlarged, and her body returned to leaning over her plate most of the time while eating. She was constantly glancing around the table. Suddenly, Lynn looked and whispered to me, "Mom is half done."

Seldom did anyone speak a word during lunch except Lynn. Lynn just would not stop talking. Suddenly, she wanted the family to know she had forgiven everyone. It was a silent moment. I glanced around the room, seeing people looking back with a blank look on their faces.

Suddenly, all hell broke out from Lynn. She broke down, sobbing and telling everyone she was so sorry for everything, including taking drugs. She just poured out her heart to the family.

I notice her father just stared at Lynn. There was no sign of love in his eyes! As I kept glancing in his direction, he just kept watching her weep. Perhaps he had never seen his little girl act like this before, or maybe he had seen it several times. After all, Lynn said her parents had taken her out of their will at least three times while she was living the wild life. Now I had a clearer understanding why Lynn told me, "We are a very private family." An acquaintance once said, "It's nobody's business what a person goes through." Sometimes that is true. Other times a person needs another person's shoulder.

Yes, my dearest diary, this was a very private family, and I highly respected their privacy. So I am only writing about a few conversations we had over a period of time together. What a person is in public is not always what that person is at home. Sometimes a person puts on a big front, but behind closed doors the individual is not the same person.

It seemed like Lynn kept everyone to a large degree on edge, including me. My heart sank as I looked around the luncheon table. I noticed there was one woman who rolled her eyes as she listened to Lynn talk. Another relative was eating very slowly. Others played with their food while some just kept their thoughts to themselves. As for me, I wanted to place a gag over Lynn's mouth.

Looking back at that day, I really think Lynn went through several personalities during the short eight hours. Even one person said, "I've seen this many times." What a very sad day. Their minds were on Tom, not Lynn. Lynn kept the conversation on herself. Everyone cared so deeply for Tom in their individual ways. Each family member was so special. Lynn might have thought that this was a private family, but that day they allowed a common stranger to see each of their hearts. What a very caring, good, and loving family.

Lunch was followed by long goodbyes and another silent drive back to the family home. Tom seemed relieved. He retreated back to his recliner and looked out the big bay window while listening to his classical music. Lynn asked me to stay and visit for a while. She looked exhausted. The caregiver was preparing for her husband to pick her up. The other caregiver had not arrived.

Lynn asked the caregiver to take a break and join us at the family dining room table. Lynn dominated the conversation, and we all reminisced a little about the past couple of years. She asked her papa to help sing a song with the words "Chick chick chickadee." We liked seeing Tom and Lynn sing together. Then we all started to laugh. This good laugh helped lighten up that day's stressful situations and hopefully released many past hurts.

Lynn spoke about how upset her mother would become when she would forget her table manners when she was a child. Lynn said it was the glint in her mom's eyes as she looked so stern that gave away her secrets of inner laughter.

Then she asked us if we ever saw a human waterfall. We just shook our heads no. Lynn grabbed my water bottle, took a huge gulp, swished it around in her mouth, put the bottle to her ear, and then squirted the water out of her mouth high into the air and onto the floor. For a moment the caregiver and I just stared as Lynn. Suddenly, we all had a very hearty laugh. We needed that sound again. The room was filled with general conversations. Good timing.

Thinking back, no one cleaned up the water. The caregiver's husband arrived, and Lynn said, "Thanks for coming." As soon as she returned to the table, Lynn gingerly commented, "Well, Mom must be totally done by now."

I was about to leave when Lynn asked me to remain for a little while longer. We checked on Tom, who had returned to his own world of music. He looked relaxed and paid no attention to the surroundings. Lynn said that we did not have much time and motioned for me to move fast with her.

We dashed downstairs. Her mother would do the same thing. Of course, living in the same home for fifty years, the owners would know how to dash up and down those steep stairs. Meanwhile, Lynn must have been looking for something. She kept looking through the basement to see what needed cleaning. She asked me to help her clean the family home when her papa left for his eternal vacation. Otherwise, she would hire a company to take everything away after her papa left to be with her mother. I told Lynn that if she needed help, I would be there for her. That's what friends are for. My dearest diary, her eyes and face looked relieved. Wasn't there anyone else who would be there to help Lynn clean everything out of the family home?

The storage room was next. Anita would often go into the storage room, so they had to block off the door. We cleared stuff away and opened the door. I glanced around and noticed stacks and stacks and more stacks of boxes filled with books, nicely stacked papers, shoes packed together, cooking pots, boxes marked "holiday," and household items lined up on the neatly placed shelves. It was no wondered Lynn had said, "I'll burn all the books." She was totally fed up with being around books. And yet everything was so well sorted and labeled. It reminded me of my home's storage area that I needed to clean up and even downsize. Lynn smiled and said, "Next room." What was Lynn looking for?

This next room was her mother's private writing room. Fishing pictures hung on the wall. Lynn had the key and asked me, "Did my mother ever mentioned or show you her typing room?" I responded with a "No." There was no need to leave the living room except when I was asked to pick up her mother's books or when I said hello to her papa in the TV room.

Lynn looked around and noticed an old typewriter, which she later passed on to me. "I remember my mom clicking on the typewriter all through the night. I would sleep on the couch until she was ready to go to bed." I asked Lynn what the family planned to do with her mother's papers, which were sprawled all around the tiny room. She answered with a hearty laugh. "Toss it! Burn it, baby. Burn it!" Did she not understand the value of these? These were her mother's thoughts on paper. Perhaps Lynn had had enough of her mother's writings after locating those two brown bags. On the other hand, I knew her mother loved the outdoors and enjoyed fishing, but her mother's papers must mean something to her family.

"Well, if no one else wants them, I'll take them and sort them out and then hand them back to you." Lynn looked at me and reached for a small red container. "Here let me know what you find." The red container had groups of different fishing places to explore with names of man-made rivers, stores where one could purchase fishing gear, places to look for the best travel agents for day trips, and even a few fishing jokes written in long hand. The one joke I liked reading, "Your fish was how long?"

It reminded me of going fishing and catching the longest fish while I was dating my hubby. This was before we were serious. Those men were so surprised. I even learned how to clean a fish. Or should I say gut a fish? Lynn told me to keep the container or burn it. Then she laughed and told me that someday I was bound to learn about fishing from what her mother wrote since she was my mentor. Was she being sarcastic?

Next, she handed me an armful of loose papers. "Tell me what these papers are about." I quickly glanced through the loose papers. It turned out Anita wrote about a young teenager who loved to go hiking and skip rocks while her papa fished. It upset Lynn when I told her the character's name. "That's me she was writing about! Why didn't she write my name?" Lynn shouted. Did the character's name really upset her that much?

We hurried upstairs to the kitchen area. "My mom would want you, as her 'other daughter,' to have her cookbooks." I was not sure if Lynn was making a slam about me being the other daughter or if she really meant it as a compliment. She located a box and filled it with *all* of her mother's cookbooks. Maybe the caregivers were using some of the cookbooks. That didn't matter to Lynn. I followed her as we walked together through the kitchen to the pantry area.

I informed Lynn to remember that I did very little cooking and could not even follow a recipe. Lynn bellowed, reminding me that she did not like to cook either. I promised her that I would start learning to cook and even try creating something myself since her mother developed several fishing cookbooks. And I have been keeping my promise.

This is my very own marinated sauce for various types of meats that produce a wonderful flavor. I have never tried it with fish.

JJ Janice

Steak with Sautéed Onions and Garlic

Serving Size: 2
Prep Time: 10 minutes
Cooking Time: 10 minutes

Ingredients

- 2 Tbsp. Avocado Oil
- 3 Tbsp. Margarine
- 1 Clove of Garlic, Crushed
- 1 Tbsp. Ground Black Pepper
- 1 Sweet Onion-Minced or Pulverized in a Food Processor
- 2 T-Bone Steaks, medium-size

Method

Warm the avocado oil and margarine in a large pan over medium heat.

Add the garlic and onion to the pan along with the black pepper to taste.

Pierce the steaks with the tip of a knife.

Add the steaks to the pan, and immediately spoon some of the onion mixture over the steaks.

Cover the pan and allow to cook for 3–5 minutes.

Turn the meat over, and repeat the process.

Cook the meat till done to personal taste.

    The two ladies would be very proud of me, and I am very proud of myself for creating my own recipe.

We kept walking into the hallway by the kitchen. There was an open wall that had been converted into an open pantry. It had shelves for canned goods and some books.

Lynn located more books. She asked, "Are there any books here you would like?" I glanced at the books and commented that her mother had once brought out an egg book to give to me. I told Lynn that I mentioned to her mother that the egg book was so beautiful, but then I said that Lynn should see if the family would like it. It was titled *Faberge Imperial Eggs and Other Fantasies* (Hermione Waterfield and Christopher Forbes, Bramhall House, 1980 Edition).

Ever since receiving this book, I've starting gathering special creative eggs and boxes of all types. It is a wonderful hobby and one that has developed with deep meanings. None of the eggs or boxes is worth anything because they usually come from the dollar store or other thrift stores. Anita, Lynn, and I all loved shopping at the same type of stores, yet I don't ever remember seeing Anita and Lynn. It's amazing what great qualities these various stores offer to the public. A price can be very low, but the quality of the item can be high. Some of the items are brand new. Maybe these two ladies liked garage sales too.

Next, we walked to the bathroom. I glanced around, but I could not figure out why she had brought me into this small room. She glanced around the mirror area, and on the wall was a needlepoint. "I made this needlepoint for my mother many years ago while living on the East Coast. I know that she would want you to have it." Lynn said it was one of the precious gifts she had made by hand for her mother. Now she wanted me to have it. Why? Lynn should have taken it home and kept this precious needlepoint.

She removed the handcrafted needlepoint and handed it to me. It appeared she had absolutely no connection to it. I remember how Anita had passed her wonderful books to me and how her last action was tenderly stretching out her arm and placing her hand on the books. She closed her eyes while touching the books. Was she giving a simple prayer of thanks for all those wonderful times reading and the educational books that gave life to her students?

JJ Janice

Some people place more value on items than others. To read the needlepoint is still very pleasing to my eyes.

When we passed the music area, Lynn and I stopped and looked at some of the records—waltzes by Richard Rogers, symphonies by Strauss, big bands with Jimmy Dorsey, singers like Jim Nabors and Wayne Newton, just to mention a few.

We laughed and conversed about our musical likes—country singers George Strait, Loretta Lynn, Patsy Cline, and Glen Campbell. I mentioned Chicago, The Beatles, Tom Jones, gravel-voice Janis Joplin, Cher, The Mamas and Papas, and Barbra Streisand. Lynn said she enjoyed singers like Carole King. I mentioned how I loved Broadway hit musicals like *South Pacific* and *Paint Your Wagon*. In our younger days, we enjoyed piano and jazz while we were out on hot dates over dinner or a glass of wine.

I asked her if she ever watched Jimmy Swaggart, a wonderful evangelist who had his own TV network. Some of the oldie Christian songs they sang were also sung by Elvis and the Mormon Tabernacle Choir. We had so much fun trying to sing some of these various artists' songs. We sounded like we were singing in the shower. Our audience at karaoke would definitely not have a good time listening to us sing. We didn't have time to come up with names for all of our wonderful singers and musicians that had brought us great memories. There were so many to mention. While backing out of the driveway the last time Lynn came to our home, she turned her music on so loud that I could hear her playing Carole King as she drove away.

My dearest diary, I felt like Anita was walking with Lynn and me that precious afternoon and encouraging us to laugh and share our thoughts on life.

Chapter 12

Lynn

Lynn was so relieved that her mom no longer faced Alzheimer's. Lynn's goal was to be this very private family's leader. She knew her mother was in heaven, and that gave her peace in her heart.

Lynn believed she came from good stock. It was imperative for her family to know her life had changed over the past couple of months—especially being married to her wonderful supportive husband. She was a person who remembered values, loved surprises and laughter, and had a heart that reached out to help others. Most importantly, she loved her hubby and wanted to spend more time with him. But the responsibility for her parents were taking its toll on her body.

Her whole attitude was changing for the better. Lynn realized her mother's importance beyond the family and how the public responded positively to her mother's books. She noticed how the beauty of her father's life positively helped other people appreciate life in other countries besides helping people to study Spanish, Chinese, Russian, French, and many other languages before they left on world travel trips. Lynn didn't really think about her parents' travels and their occupations. They were just her parents. But going through her mother's belongings was a real eye-opener. Lynn started to see how their lives made a position impact on people from around the world.

Lynn had promised her mother she would no longer smoke. It was really important to Lynn that she keep her word. She tried to do it alone. Late one night in one of her depressed moods, she fell on her knees and met Jesus face-to-face. She actually *saw Him* standing by her side. He wiped away her tears and reached out to touch her hand. Gladly, she accepted His hand, and together they talked. Lynn said it was the greatest high she ever experienced.

She understood the word *forgiveness* and wanted to do the same in her life. The next day she went to a jewelry store and purchased a gold cross. Lynn said, "It feels good." She even phoned me on Easter morning. It's what Christians do. She explained the importance of following through on forgiveness. That week her father saw the cross around her neck, but he did not ask her about it. Instead he asked me how long Lynn had been wearing it. I answered, "Lynn accepted Jesus last week. She went out and purchased a cross." Her papa appeared very pleased.

Lynn sought peace among family members. She wanted to break the curse of family separation and negative attitudes, and it started with herself. Through her determination and desire for leadership, I noticed Lynn's heart was sincerely reaching out for the family's forgiveness. She wanted the family to unify. I admired her.

She placed value on each family member for being who she or he was. She loved and admired her special man. She had her ups and downs, but the bottom line was that being this man's wife was her real life. This was her man. He loved her, and he had stood beside her for so many years. Oh, how she dearly loved her superman. She knew this was the key man in her life. She had found true love. As wives, we spoke about marriage and knowing the real meaning of happiness.

Lynn spoke about moving out of the family home as soon as she graduated. Lynn had proclaimed that she was on her own. Years later this very gifted lady was ashamed that she had not furthered her education after high school. Several times Lynn repeated that her whole life changed when she chose to smoke marijuana in her late teens. It started a spiral downhill with drugs, and she had a very hard time controlling her desire for highs. Some people don't need an extra high and can stick with marijuana, but that wasn't Lynn's fate.

Lynn really wanted to change her lifestyle so that her parents would be proud of her, but the hidden drugs in her bloodstream urged her to return to self-medicating at times. Lynn chose to go cold turkey several times, hoping to become free from the drugs attacking her body over and over again. But she was jailed for drugs, received DUIs, and drank alcohol. Plus there were not very many places she could work because of her misadventures and life decisions.

She served mostly as a trusted bartender in taverns in order to pay the bills. Life was not easy because of her past choices. But she could pay the bills, and she even had some extra money to enjoy a hobby. Skydiving was expensive, but so much fun. The first time she went skydiving alone, she landed on a garage roof. The people watched her drop from the open blue sky, land safely on their garage roof, rustled up a ladder, and then helped her off the landing pad. They invited Lynn to their party. She liked the party but never wanted to land on a roof ever again because she might hurt herself or meet a family who didn't think it was funny.

Lynn was a lady filled with the zest of life. As an intelligent person, she could have chosen many different type of employment—psychologist, photographer, writer, artist, teacher, veterinarian, horse trainer, businesswoman, geologist—and the list could go on and on because Lynn was a talented person.

Instead Lynn made some very poor choices. She really wanted to earn a degree. She knew her parents would pay for the university expenses, but how did a person who had once been incarcerated attend a university? She never expressed a desire for a specific degree to me, but she really wanted to have it. I am not sure if her parents ever knew or realized how much Lynn wanted to earn a degree, perhaps even get her master's or her doctorate.

Lynn was unpredictable most of the time, seeking out life's adventures. She loved playing jokes and telling funny stories. Once she told me how she woke up her husband. They crawled on the floor through the living room because she thought there was a burglar. When they reached the front door area, she jumped up and yelled, "April fools!" Of course, her hubby knew their home had security lights, and the lights weren't showing. What a wonderful man for loving Lynn for who she was.

Her dream was to be accepted for who she was. Perhaps we all want to be accepted for who we are, what we think, or what our lives are like. No one can change anyone. Only God can work in a person's heart. After Lynn accepted Jesus into her heart, she truly repented and looked at life with a positive and hopeful future.

She started to see the seriousness of being a daughter and wife. There is a difference between being a daughter who wants to show she can handle responsibilities and being a daughter who responds with love. Some feel obliged, and others care for parents from their hearts. I'm not sure which Lynn did, but I am sure that she loved her parents very much.

Lynn did not hold any important public roles like her parents had, yet she loved people and especially animals. She wanted to surprise her hubby with a dream come true, so when she came into some inheritance, Lynn immediately purchased him his own special motorcycle. She loved the family dog and talked about moving somewhere with acreage and a fishing lake. She hoped to be able to have her own mini ranch with her hubby. By purchasing a farm, they'd have the freedom to jump rocks by their lake, fish all day, watch a cow graze on healthy green grass, gather eggs, and even keep a horse or two, though they knew that having a horse could become very expensive. She had loved horses since she was a teenager. Lynn never grew out of wanting to own her own horse.

Sadly, Lynn's body was worn down from all the drugs, alcohol, and smoking during previous years. Real life was catching up with her abused body. She had stopped drinking and using drugs years earlier, but it was that black tar from smoking that eventually filled her lungs. She couldn't breathe very easy anymore. Of course, she still smoked. Lynn gave herself ten to fifteen years to live. Then she figured her lungs would give up life. However, the day of her mother's cremation service, Lynn looked like she had lost so much weight that her face almost resembled a skeleton.

By listening to Anita and watching Lynn, I learned that we must make the most out of life each day. We must love from the depths of our heart and realize there must be forgiveness. Love stands up for what is right and does not get hung up on negatives. Life includes laughing and being open. It is important to believe that every person has a purpose, even if it's only to be true to oneself. Perhaps part of Lynn's life's purpose was to help people see value in themselves, be happy, and live life to the fullest. Perhaps it was her way to help me remember that there is forgiveness and that every life is important. Live life with a purpose! Lynn would have loved you, my dearest diary. She loved people, but Lynn did have her highs and lows.

It was Memorial Day weekend, and I received a message from Lynn.

Message dated 5/23/07 2:17 PM (Partial email)

JJ, please have a wonderful Memorial Day weekend. Things are just really weird for me. Life is like a machine gun, one thing after another after another and then all of a sudden it all stopped. I do not know what to do with myself. Please try and understand. After being almost overpowered with such profound emotion, all of a sudden I just feel nothing. It is kind of like the band stopped playing or something… weir d. Lynn

The following weekend when I was driving home from vacationing in Nebraska, I received a phone call from the caregiver. When I received the news, I screamed, "No! No! No!" The caregiver kept saying, "Yes! Yes! Yes!" I was so shocked hearing that Lynn had suddenly passed away.

Apparently, she had been trying to email someone the night before. Why had her home's electricity been cut off during that horrible windstorm? No one will ever know who she was trying to contact. Perhaps she was depressed and seeking help. Hopefully, she intended to send that last email to her hubby. I sure do hope so. But no one will ever know.

I told the caregiver I would arrive at the family home in about three hours. The family was so sweet. Everyone was still there when I arrived.

My mind kept racing because it had been four short months since her mother's death. How could this tragedy happen?

Just before leaving on our vacation, Lynn and I had had an extremely serious falling out over her papa. A day earlier while I was on vacation, the caregiver contacted me to see if I would phone Lynn because she was very worried about Lynn's health. I told the caregiver that Lynn hated me and did not want any further contact. It was a bad choice on my part.

Even if Lynn would not have answered my phone call or if she had hung up when she heard my voice, I could have phoned and left a message. Maybe it would have made a difference. But when a person's time is up, there's probably no way of holding up the departure date. Can death be cheated?

I've read stories about people saved from a devastating disaster like a train wreck, not taking an airplane at the last minute, or even escaping an overturned car and living to tell their story. Could what saved them be a mother's prayer or angels watching over them?

Sometimes people really do not mean what they say. Words cannot be taken back once they are spoken. There's a simple saying *Sticks and stones may break my bones, but words can never hurt me.* That's not true. Bones can repair themselves, but words can be like sharp knives cutting deep into a person's mind and heart. Tears can bleed all over a pillow. Only love can overshadow ill-spoken words.

I had told Lynn that it was just fine with me if we went our separate ways because my promise had been to her mother, not her father or her. Lynn told me that I was no longer welcome to visit her father because he was her papa and she would take care of him. It was okay for me to care about her mother and even be the *other daughter*, but her father was her papa. I couldn't understand all this anger from Lynn. I had my own dad. I did not need her dad. She just could not relate to what I was saying. Her papa was a very lonely man, so I offered him some homemade cookies. *So what?* I've done this for other people—relatives, friends, neighbors, and even coworkers.

When I asked Lynn about baking some cookies for her father, she asked me if I did this for other people too. I even named a few so that she knew I wasn't interfering with her family. I know friends who do this same thing. However, Lynn just could not accept this, and her response was enough for me to toss her to the wind.

I told this story again to the caregiver over the phone. I had baked some chocolate chip cookies and asked Lynn if it was okay for me to bring them to her lonely papa. At that time Lynn gave her permission. When I visited her father, we talked about fishing from rocks compared to fishing from a boat. We talked about my thirtyseven-pound salmon that was more than three feet long. It was a very simple conversation. This upset Lynn because I had no right to have this type of conversation with her father. *What?* What is wrong with this type of conversation?

But when it came to Lynn, she had her highs when she was pleased to have me take cookies to her papa, and she had her lows when he was her papa and hers alone. I became very impatient, not caring about our friendship.

The previous week during one of our phone calls, Lynn mentioned that while she was visiting her papa, he had slapped her hand *really hard* when she reached for his candy. She was totally shocked, and she blamed me. You see, the candy was from one of my previous trips. I usually brought simple goodies back with me when traveling to share with other people. However, when her papa hit her hand, Lynn's heart broke.

She reminded me that sometimes a little child seeks to be accepted and loved. Her elderly father's discipline devastated this caring daughter's heart. Why did he really slap her hand? She loved sharing and joking, but this time it backfired. Lynn said his look was so stern. It was the first time he had ever reprimanded her jokes. Lynn told me her papa would always stand up for her when she was a child. There were no excuses, but he would take her side when she did something wrong. As for her mother, it was right or wrong.

My mind reviewed how, why, and even when a person could forgive ugly thoughts that often return. Why do they keep returning? She could not get his look or the slap out of her mind. That old devil just kept sending demons to taunt her and ruin day after day after day. No one can take back ugly words or bad actions. One time this mouthy person was visiting our home and wanted to talk with my hubby while he was watching TV. Lynn walked in front of the TV and stomped on my hubby's toes. After that, my hubby had no use for this person. My hubby has diabetes, and after stomping on his toes, he became worried about the feeling in his feet. Even when Lynn would say goodbye to him, he seldom responded back. She sensed this, but I know she didn't realize how disrespectful she had been. The two of them shared no more conversations.

What about when people repent and say they are sorry because they really didn't mean what they said or the action presented? Well, maybe Lynn really didn't mind me baking some cookies for her papa and her. That previous vacation evening after thinking about what the caregiver had said, I changed my mind. I would contact Lynn after I arrived home from vacation. Real friendship will forgive, and maybe we could have some more laughs or go to a funny movie about animals. We wouldn't see each other on Sunday afternoons, but just maybe we could meet every other month or a couple of times a year and have lunch together. It might take time, but hopefully, there was some friendship left between us. I didn't take the caregiver seriously about Lynn's bad health.

In fact, the last evening on vacation looking around in a nearby variety store, I purchased a small brown teddy bear. I would mail it to Lynn and tell Lynn how proud I was of her for keeping her word to her mother to stop smoking. The note would say that she was missed, but I would honor her wishes and not visit her lonely father or contact her again until she contacted me. I hoped that this time she would not mutilate this bear like the second bear that I had given her. Perhaps she would return this package. I would take my chances.

My thoughts returned to the time when her mother passed away and I handed Lynn another brown bear. I thought she might like another one. Wrong! Lynn informed me that the day after she received the second bear, she looked at it and didn't like the eyes, so she mutilated it, stuffed it in a brown bag, and buried it six feet deep in the ground. She liked the first bear, but this other bear made her upset. Was she really talking about me? Did she relate her anger to me visiting her father and then take her rage out on that bear? Was this part of her bipolar disorder? What else would she do? Why should I give her another bear? Maybe it represented forgiveness and caring. Was the *other* bear really a reference to me? Did she want to eliminate me?

My mind thought about how much longer her papa could bear his wife's empty space. Lynn expected to hear any day from his caregiver that her father had joined her mother in heaven. Instead her papa received one last surprise, learning of Lynn's death. How much more could he take?

I smiled, thinking back to a time just several weeks earlier when Lynn had come up with an idea to cheer up her papa. She brought all his service friends who were still alive to their home for food and conversations. As usual, like her mother, Lynn was full of life. She developed this reunion's fabulous idea all on her own.

The living room was filled with great conversations about old times. Lynn notified me that it had been one great tearjerker of a time for the family. Lynn loved surprising people. Sometimes she just liked shocking people so that she could see their reactions, especially mine. She must have had some bellowing laughs about me.

Sometimes it is better to swallow your pride. You can never turn back the hands of time. Because I hesitated, I can never tell Lynn how special she was to her hubby, papa, family, and me. I honored her request not to contact her or her family ever again. There are times when it is far better to remove yourself from contacting a person, but in this case perhaps it was wrong that I didn't listen closer to the caregiver.

It was time to continue to move forward. I felt I had given my all. I started to visualize what the family's forgiveness must have meant to Lynn. The past really did not matter. We only need to forgive and to say, "I love you."

What is the real meaning of forgiveness? What is the real meaning of love? Years ago I read and cut out a short article titled "The Art of Forgiving" by Eda LeShan. I do not even remember what magazine it came from or the date. It said that forgiving others' shortcomings is easy once you've learned to forgive your own. The article talks about how in order to forgive another person, that person must find the root of his or her own problem. I realized Lynn really longed for and needed assurance that her parents loved her. She longed to be forgiven and accepted by them. That is why it was vitally important that her mother turned back into her loving mom even if for a few moments in time together. Lynn was ecstatically happy to have heard her mom speak slowly those precious words, "I love you." These three simple words were refreshing to Lynn's ears and heart.

I would regret my procrastination in telling Lynn I cared about her. A moment of time had passed me by. To this day, I remember how special each season of life has become. I make sure that most people know they are greatly appreciated.

During those three hours traveling back home from vacation, I could not forgive myself for abandoning Lynn and not contacting her that previous day. When I arrived at the family home, condolences were passed on to Lynn's hubby and Tom. I didn't know what to say to Lynn's hubby. He looked totally devastated, and maybe giving him a hug would show him I cared. Meanwhile, Tom was sitting in his recliner, escaping from reality while listening to his music. His eyes were so red, and he looked exhausted. Yes, he could retreat into his own simple world of music and look out the big bay window and watch the fishing boats. The elderly end up forgetting what day it is because every day usually has the same routine; however, this was not any ordinary day. This gave me some peace of mind, knowing Tom could enjoy his music.

I stayed for about an hour. Tom came out on the patio to eat with everyone. He asked, "Where's JJ?" Someone must have said I was sitting by the back door. My heart sank, and finally, I had to say goodbye to everyone. Lynn's hubby said he would leave with me. I felt honored that I could walk out with Lynn's superman. As I looked around, I saw that my sorrow was nothing compared to what the immediate family was experiencing.

As we were leaving, I stopped where Tom was sitting and gave him a farewell hug. I forgot about Tom's hearing aids. I gave him a hug, kissed his cheek, and then told him quietly in his ear, "I love you." But his hearing aids were turned up loud, and they gave a very loud shrilling noise that turned his red eyes into bug eyes. I apologized to Tom, but his eyes were still big as I walked away. I thought the people around us were going to fall off their chairs and drop to the floor laughing. That was one bad laugh on me.

When Lynn's husband and I were walking toward his car, I asked for a special request. It was an extremely bad time to ask for something, but it might be the only time I'd have. I wanted something with which to remember his beloved Lynn. He simply asked, "What would you like?"

I replied, "Is it all right with you if I could have the brown teddy bear riding in the back seat of your car?" He didn't even realize there was a teddy bear that was buckled in the back seat! He unbuckled the teddy bear and handed it to me. I'm sure family members were already asking for some of Lynn's belonging, and I felt guilty requesting that bear; however, I figured no one would know the background of that first brown bear that caught so many of Lynn's tears. Now both that teddy bear and the very small teddy bear from Nebraska are together.

Lynn loved hard. She fought the devil himself and came out my champion. We can't take any money, education, rewards, or material possessions to heaven. We take our attitudes and love in our heart. Many times Lynn was off the wall with her bipolar disorder, but she had a heart full of gold. She cared about other people. Her heart gave more joy than anyone could count, especially in regards to her parents and hubby.

She no longer would need to hang her head in shame, remembering her times with drugs, jail, and drinking. Those years were long gone. The devil and demons who attacked her system were no longer in control. Lynn achieved the golden rule in learning to forgive her own self and others by accepting Jesus in her life. Belonging to her superman was all she needed to bring a smile to her face. She was aware that love came from hearts and vows.

A couple of days later in the late afternoon, one of the family members asked if I would drive Tom and the caregiver to Lynn's funeral service. That tedious memorial day, I brought my camera, but the family members informed me there would be *no* pictures. I supposed the way Lynn had created a memorial book about Anita was too much for the entire family. It really was somewhat gruesome.

Perhaps that's why the family sought peaceful memories in place of taking pictures for this event. In Lynn's defense, when I was growing up, these were the same types of pictures that were taken at funerals and handed out to family members. However, the pictures that were taken at Anita's cremation were quite a bit detailed.

I understood the family's concern regarding Lynn. Maybe they were afraid that I would make up some memory album for them in regards to Lynn. Her picture album of her mother's cremation day was enough to last me a lifetime.

It was nice seeing the family again, but not under these circumstances. Lynn's funeral had an open casket. Her whole family was there, and I believe all of us were still in total shock, including me. What can one say to a grieving husband? That she longed to be the wife she knew he deserved? What does a person say to a papa who now has another huge void in his life and heart? Who will come visit him? Everyone lived so far away.

I asked permission to place something in her casket, and the family said I could. Lynn loved the American flag and her mother's Bible. Several weeks earlier on a Sunday afternoon, she stopped by our home to show me she had located her mother's Bible. Lynn told me that she was reading it late at night, but the instances of thee and thou were hard to understand. The next week when she stopped by

Entwined Hearts

our home, I handed her a young silver eagle and told her it was to help her fly as her life changed and she no longer had to care for her mother. She loved it and placed it in one of her plants. Thus, because Lynn loved her mother's Holy Bible and our country's flag, I located a very small flag and placed it along with Psalm 23 in her casket.

When it was my turn in line to view Lynn in her casket, I gently placed my finger on Lynn's forehead and gave the sign of the cross. I firmly spoke, "In the name of the Father, Son, and Holy Spirit, you are Mine!" Then I told her I loved her. When I reached my finger out to place the sign of the cross on her forehead, I heard gasps. It was just a body, but the spirit needed to be blessed. Even the minister did not question why I performed this action. Lynn knew there was a real heaven.

What surprised me was the fact that Lynn had told the presiding minister at her service that she had accepted Jesus, but he said nothing about that during the funeral service. I approached the minister after the service and asked him why he didn't tell the family about Lynn's spiritual awareness. Wasn't this service to honor the deceased? Why was it only him and me saying the Lord's Prayer and no one else? Why didn't he tell her life story, seeing Jesus and accepting Him as her Savior? But it was a very nice service.

I remember when my father passed away. All that pastor could say over and over was how wonderful my father's chili tasted and how everyone would miss that chili. He was a faithful husband and good father, and he provided for his family. He attended church regularly and served on committees. Just because we sat in the back of the church and didn't have a lot of money to place into the Sunday collection plate didn't make him only a good chili chef for church events.

Watching TV evangelists has been good for me because I now feel that I don't need to face people's judgment within churches any longer. I love Bible studies and prayer groups like the one led by Marilyn Hickey. Then there are Christian organizations like Morris Cerullo World Evangelism and John Hagee Ministries that give me energy. I love reading about the Make-a-Wish program and St.

Jude Hospital. I seek out positive TV programs where I can hear or at least imagine those simple words, "I love you."

What a beautiful lady and woman Lynn was. She lived life the best she could. May she always be remembered for her beautiful heart and the love she had for her hubby and parents. I hope that she is looking down from heaven and that she knows she was appreciated.

I've heard people in heaven can see us and can communicate with us. I know that Anita has repeated to me, "Shoulders back, head up. Stop sniffling. Move forward!" I've even heard Anita's voice. It's kind of creepy yet so sweet for our loved ones to communicate with us from their eternal resting place. There is life after death.

One of my coworkers once said that she would see a feather float down from the sky sometimes when she was walking. There were no trees, bushes, or birds nearby, just a single feather that floated close for her to catch. The feather was from her husband, who had passed away several years earlier. When he was alive, he would give her a feather for good luck. It was his thing to do for her.

I hope Lynn is smiling and happy seeing me penning *Entwined Hearts*. I'm sure it would inspire her heart to see that her life had a purpose. The purpose perhaps was for you, my dearest diary, to learn about Lynn's life and realize that there is forgiveness when a person reaches out to accept Jesus. Life continues no matter what happens. As one pastor said many years ago, "What is truth is truth, no matter what one believes." There is life beyond this world. I know that you are not real, but you are still my dearest diary.

May both Anita's and Lynn's zeal for life inspire others to live on and remember one another. I deeply miss these ladies. They listened, and they were full of wisdom. As for Lynn, I loved when she would tell me about playing jokes, when she shocked people, and when she reached out to walk arm in arm with me. Sometimes at night I will wake up, and my cheeks will have tears on them because I was dreaming of seeing Anita and Lynn again. I must face reality and accept that I will see them again in heaven and not down here on earth. They made a very strong impact on my life. Believe in yourself. You have talents and skills, so have self-confidence to reach out in life.

I heard that Lynn died of pneumonia, which is what Anita died from too. Pneumonia is an illness that doctors can clear up with medicine if they catch it in time. I have asked myself, "Why didn't Lynn go to the doctor?" One of our conversations was about doctors. She mentioned a time when her arm tattoo became infected. Her doctor told her she needed to take all of her antibiotics to fight the infection and that she had to prevent people from touching the new tattoo. Perhaps she did not want to face her doctor and ask him for more medicines.

My mind no longer races for answers. I understood that smoking for more than forty years, Lynn's lungs were not in the best of shape. I cannot even imagine the pain and deep loss her husband must have gone through, knowing the illness that took her life might have been prevented.

We will see each other in heaven. We will walk beside the still waters and on streets paved with gold. We will laugh and sing and dance together walking arm in arm in the land of no tears. We will face God Almighty, the Heavenly Father, and thank Him for these precious seasons, serving Him in His glory. We will have a clearer understanding to the true meaning of Jesus dying on the cross and the power of the Holy Spirit and angels in our lives. He is very merciful.

Chapter 13

Can't Handle Any More

Anita and Lynn moved forward to their eternal vacations within four months of each other. I was there as a witness when poor Tom looked at Lynn in her coffin and tears rolled down his red cheeks, saying, "I can't take any more." Unlike Anita's service, Lynn had no pictures. It was as though she didn't exist after the service. Unlike the quiet luncheon after Anita's service, Lynn's luncheon overflowed with conversations and even laughter. My mind was so glad this family was together and that the father heard the conversations and laughter. It made my heart sing.

Returning that afternoon to the family home, Tom was able to escape back into his musical world, sitting in his recliner by the big bay window. That afternoon he didn't look up to watch the boats through the binoculars. Lynn's papa only looked down at his tightly folded fingers, showing his white knuckles. The devastation showed all over his withdrawn face. This emotionally wounded man was beyond loneliness. Now he was faced with two empty spaces in his life. Even his music could not replace the immense voids.

My dearest diary, the stress and loneliness created a huge void in Tom's life, so I stepped forward. I asked the extended family's permission to visit with Tom once a week. They granted me this privilege and opportunity.

The first Wednesday after Lynn's funeral, I promised Tom I would come see him; however, I forgot that I needed to travel to

Entwined Hearts

South Dakota. Driving back, I received a phone call from the caregiver asking when I planned to arrive to visit Tom. They had been waiting all afternoon for me to visit Tom. I gasped. I was disappointed in myself for not communicating my travel plans. She reminded me that continuity was the backbone of an elderly person's daily routine. They might have an appointment, but very few people came to visit. She educated me about the importance of remembering to visit because it broke up the normal day's activities and the elderly person looked forward to that day's change. I was still useful to this family. God could use me to help this elderly man remember that people cared about him and loved him. He would not be forgotten.

A promised was made to visit Tom that next week and to bring some homemade cookies that we could share together. I requested that the caregiver ask Tom if he would prefer chocolate chip cookies or oatmeal cookies… or both. Tom answered, "Chocolate chip cookies."

He liked food, so the following week I brought him a cheeseburger, fries, and more homemade chocolate chip cookies. We sat at the kitchen table and enjoyed simple conversations with the delicious food.

The third week I asked Tom if he liked Peruvian food. His eyes lit up, and a big smile spread across his face. The extended family was invited to come and be together with Tom as if the occasion was a family gathering. What a very special luncheon. Everyone came. We had some laughs and great conversations. The men wheeled Tom around the property so he could have a look at the lawn, flowers, and shrubs. Tom mentioned that the shrubbery needed some trimming. Perhaps it was his time to say goodbye to everyone, including his home. What a very happy memorable day for everyone.

That following week Tom passed away. I felt privileged that I had been invited to his home that day. A family member asked if I would like to view Tom before the funeral personnel picked him up.

I immediately went to his bedroom. It was good to thank Tom for allowing me into his home to visit his wife and him. I thanked him for the simple conversations and allowing me to bring him delicious foods for several weeks. Then like Anita and Lynn, I placed my finger on his forehead and gave the sign of the cross. I firmly spoke, "In the name of the Father, Son, and Holy Spirit, you are Mine!" I told him I loved him and thanked him again. I kissed his forehead as I had done with Anita. Years later I came to the realization even a common stranger can be utilized by God Almighty to claim a person for the Lord. I'm no priest. I'm just God's humble servant.

The caregiver was in the doorway. She listened to every word. The caregiver said that she needed to know how I was connected with this family. Funny how there are people who just need to know, but they still don't understand why people come into the lives of other people. I hoped she would be my lifetime friend. She came from Europe. When I asked, "Did Anita, Tom, and you ever talk about your travels?" the caregiver replied, "Never." It baffled me, realizing how three people had so much traveling in common yet shared no conversations regarding the countries they had explored. Just because someone is hired to work for a family doesn't mean they have nothing in common with them.

Once again, I was asked to drive to Tom's service. Sadly, only the caregiver and I were in the car. How different it was with just us driving together compared to the first time with Lynn, her hubby, the caregiver, Tom, and me attending Anita's cremation. Then a second service less than four months later with only Tom, the caregiver, and me driving to Lynn's funeral. Now only the caregiver and I were driving to Tom's service a month later.

Tom's service was different. Honor guards were present, and both his and his beloved wife's ashes were placed together side by side in the cemetery. Wow! What an honor to be asked to attend this different service. This was not a private ceremony like Anita's or Lynn's service. It included military friends and associates Tom had known throughout his service life. What a caring family. The family had a potluck instead of gathering at a restaurant. The luncheon was simple, and many conversations were filled with laughter. The atmosphere was good because life was moving forward for everyone. I was very proud of this family. Anita must have taught them to hold their heads high and shoulders back. The future will always come.

This family went through so much in such a very short period of time. The stress was never ending. They allowed the caregiver and me the experience to understand three different services—cremation, open casket, and honor service. I will always remember the gun salute and the flag being folded. Lynn loved that flag because it stood for freedom, which we often take for granted. When I visited abroad, I realized the importance of green grass and open curtains. Perhaps that is partially why I loved looking out the family's large bay windows with no bars.

It was almost six months after Lynn left that I realized there had been no newspaper obituary notification written for her. It occurred to me how huge of a difference there was between honoring the image of a wealthy person who had contributed to the community versus that of the commoners like Lynn and myself.

Tom and Anita were very well educated and had earned high respect from the public locally, nationally, and worldwide. They were connected to their various worlds through writing and traveling. Plus they had invested carefully. This couple traveled the world and gave lectures on their adventures. Their activities contained concerts and operas within their community and abroad, but Lynn's past involved drugs, jail, and alcoholism. People didn't appear to have any interest in her life. I've noticed when there is an obituary, that person has the ability to influence the community or world in some way. Perhaps he or she was an entertainer or held high office. Lynn had been clean from drugs for years, but she didn't care to be a public figure like her parents. It wasn't important how long she was married or what type of work she did. She was like me, just a commoner who cared about other people who had no special titles.

I contacted Lynn's hubby to see if I had his permission to contact a newspaper reporter. He replied through an email, "Yes." Several months later an article in the local newspaper appeared about Lynn. She was probably smiling, looking down on us from heaven, realizing there had been a purpose for her life and every person born. The article was about a wonderful lady who loved life. Sometimes we just do not know or understand what our purpose is. I've thought about the article and her life. Even if it helped one person to live life with less stress and laugh more, then the article was worth every word. Maybe it helped others find life outside of their safety boxes and remember that people cared about who they were.

My dearest diary, on the other hand, because of deep stress in Lynn's life, her addiction to smoking and certain pills constantly taxed her system. Once she told me that I had no understanding of drugs. I did not know what stress really was. Nor did I have the knowledge to help her cope. She was probably right.

According to Lynn, her doctor prescribed pills that seemed to blot out emotions. Since she had many highs and lows, it was good that she utilized her doctor's prescription. I knew the difference between drugs like marijuana and cocaine compared to prescription medications, yet Lynn liked to make fun of my naivete.

Many years ago I attended a seminar on stress. I learned about Maslow's *Hierarchy of Needs*, which says that we must meet our basic needs. Everyone has the basic need to belong. When an adult does not feel that this need is met, he or she will harbor insecurity and anxiety, which leads to relationship problems. To what degree can stress be controlled when a person is bipolar and that main belonging need is not met? The person must know he or she is loved and cared about. However, the bipolar person can have all *his* or *her needs* met without the realizing how to deal with each one, especially the need to belong.

On one of my internet searches, I found a colorful chart that breaks down the five levels of belonging—self-actualization, esteem (success and status), love and belonging (affiliation and acceptance), safety needs (security and stability), and physiological needs (food, water, etc.).

This opened my eyes. I knew that Lynn's bipolar disease was part of a depression beyond my normal understanding. Lynn had been right. I was naive at least to some degree.

Grief can be coupled with stress, which enhances a deep emotional and intense journey that took over both Lynn's and Tom's lives as they dealt with Anita's Alzheimer's. Each person handles stress and grieving in their own way and own timing. People usually do not want to be victims. However, sometimes they become the victim of circumstances. In my opinion, my dearest diary, all people are human beings with a purpose. That's why we are born and given choices in life.

I learned about different symptoms associated with grieving—headaches, shortness of breath, dry mouth, skin problems, weakness in immune system, dizziness, heaviness in the chest, fatigue, changes in appetite, sensitivity to stimuli, and the list keeps going.

Tom and Lynn went through so much grief over the years, watching Anita succumb to Alzheimer's. Grief can take its toll. Living in my own box of safety and security, many times I could not relate to other people's journeys through stress, depression, grief, or even bereavement. I was surviving on a daily basis! In the aftermath of Anita's death, I picked up *The Everything Alzheimer's* book, which was so easy for me to read and understand. The information helped me fill in some missing puzzle pieces dealing with Lynn's feelings of success, highs and lows, her need to be loved, belonging, insecurity, and other personal issues. Because I lived in my comfort zone, most of my life I didn't know how to talk with Lynn. She needed a professional to help her understand.

During one of our Sunday talks, Lynn once questioned if her life would ever move forward and if she would ever gain peace dealing with Alzheimer's and her aging parents. She felt overwhelmed being so tied down to her parents! She could not forget how her parents were consuming her time. She could not forget how Alzheimer's had changed her mother's personality. Her mother forgetting her own daughter's name and shouting, "Get out," devastated Lynn. I told her, "I don't know." Life still goes on, moving forward with the clock of time.

My parents and I were not close, so when they departed from this life, there were very few tears. It wasn't the same for Lynn, who was very close to her parents. If I had the following information at that time, perhaps I could have helped Lynn. To this day, I feel guilty having lived in my safe zone for so long. I was unable to provide clear and helpful answers to her questions!

The Everything Alzheimer's book mentioned a typical timetable for grief and bereavement.

- **First month:** One is busy with responsibilities, including paperwork.
- **Third month:** One is beginning to feel the pain of loss.
- **Fourth through twelfth month:** There are good and bad days (i.e., anniversaries).
- **First-year anniversary:** One usually relives the last difficult days.
- **Second-year anniversary:** It usually takes a good two years for a person to establish a new routine and gain a new identity and lifestyle.

I also learned how grief affects areas of life like behavior and physicality. For example, people can often become defiant. Their level of responsibilities within the family sometimes changes, or they may experience things like anxiety attacks, sleep deprivation, and appetite changes. This was exactly what Lynn was going through the last month of her mother's stay at the center and the next month after her mother's death.

People may think, *Will I ever be able to move on?* Lynn was asking me this same question. Lynn experienced these types of thoughts, and it affected her physically. She relied on her hubby to keep her emotions leveled out. He was her superman, and he gave her hope and inspiration for a happy future. One night she tried to phone me. She just needed to talk to someone. It was after midnight, and my phone was shut off. Sometimes grieving makes one confused, sad, fearful, and/or angry. Often there are feelings of guilt and denial. Was this what Lynn went through when she stated that she no longer wanted me to be part of the family? She was okay with me taking homemade cookies to her father, but then she would become totally upset when I did.

I read how a grieving person includes their departed loved one in conversations and how feelings of depression can last up to and beyond a couple of years. Anniversaries are challenging since we remember that the person is no longer present. That person will be missed. A person can become fatigued and distressed. Food and activities are sometimes not at the forefront of one's mind. Was this why Lynn was losing so much weight after her mother's passing?

One of the last times I saw Lynn, she told me she couldn't handle seeing and talking with me. I looked like her mother with my white (silver) hair. My home reminded her of her parents' home because nothing matched and it was stuffed to the hilt with papers and books everywhere. What really topped it all off was how she thought I talked like her mother. She did not need to be reminded of her mother. As for her father, he would be just fine without me. And I would be fine without visiting Tom. My life could become mine again.

It hurt when Lynn informed me that my duty to the family was completed. *Duty! What duty?* I felt she just could not relate to why a person keeps a *promise*. A promise is an invitation to follow through. It's like the friend of a friend who died in the movie *Lonesome Dove*. That friend honored the request to be buried in a special place. It took months, but the request was honored.

I came to the conclusion that Lynn was just too up and down for me to even continue to consider keeping in contact. She was right. It was time to go our separate ways. My life would be so much easier to live without this person. Yes, I wanted my life back without this person's emotional drama.

So after that day's conversation and agreeing to go our own way respectfully, I walked Lynn to her car. This emotional person stopped in front of me and suddenly said, "Wait! This was Mom and Papa's favorite song." Lynn was always full of surprises. Perhaps it was the main reason that people needed a special alertness when they were around her. It was not that I needed a new friend. It was just that she gave a fresh perspective on life. It kind of intrigued me to figure out what made her love life so challenging with all of her surprises. Oh, what a very good humor God has connecting people's paths in life together for His purposes.

I smiled and told her I was her friend for life, she knew how to contact me, and she would always be welcome in our home. When the time was right for her to come back and visit, our home would be open to her.

As I was turning away from her car again, she suddenly opened her car door and instructed me, "Wait a minute. Let's finish listening to the song." It was called "I Will Never Leave You." One moment she wanted to say goodbye, and the next moment she changed her mind and wanted to share special moments together. Was this part of her bipolar disorder? It really confused me.

Then she repeated, "A con artist is always a con artist. Remember that, JJ. Never trust an ex-drug user. Watch your back because they will steal from you or ask if you have an aspirin just to check out your medicine cabinet." She was totally correct. I've experienced this, and that person takes a very long time in the bathroom. I even had some very precious items stolen by people visiting my home.

All people have stresses in their lives. How much stress a person can actually handle differs based on the level of stress.

Learning about Maslow's *Hierarchy of Needs* helped me gain a clearer understanding about basic needs. Of course, we need food, water, and shelter. But everyone also needs to give and receive love and belonging, which means establishing affiliation and acceptance within the family and community. *Self-esteem* is the way you look at yourself in terms of success and status, which is vitally important. The top need is *self-actualization*. Who are you to yourself?

Every person personally needs to realize that he or she is a real person with needs, abilities, and talents that are vital for one's success. When you (and the way other people look at you) do not see yourself as an important person who has talents and abilities, you can become silent. Who will listen? Who will see the various talents and communication skills and include you? This has been the way I have perceived myself because I lived in my safe zone and didn't allow people to actually become part of my life. Every person was considered an associate.

I've thought about the reasons our three paths crossed for a short season. Only one of us was very successful in her professional career. Yet all of us learned it was okay to step out of our own safe zone. During that time in my life, I realized that life was a continuous work of art in the making.

The Weaving of Moments

By JJ Janice

Their searching eyes no longer gaze out beyond the bay windows.

My viewing no longer showed the peering out with welcomed waves and smiles.

Our memories joining together, remembering the smiles, laughter, conversations, phone calls, visiting the family home, or holding hands. Our hearts peeling away negative remembrances, even our thoughts blacked into a void called la-la land. There will be no more walking arm in arm.

Someday our faces will meet, our arms will hold each other close, and our eyes will see our hearts overflowing with gladness and peace.

Life once again will be filled with joy and the tapestry of entwined hearts. Love will have been woven with pure love. Our arms will embrace each other with loving firmness, again uplifting each other in high esteem as our eyes view our inner depths of our hearts.

Till those precious moments reappear, "Hasta Luego" and not "Adios," for there is never to be another goodbye.

Chapter 14

Marijuana and Alcoholism

The challenges of drugs are hard enough to live with. Now mix addiction with bipolar disorder and put that face-to-face with the reality of dealing with a parent who's suffering from Alzheimer's. I could see how it would turn a beautiful daughter's life into depression at times. Where is the purpose in this person's life? What does it mean to be a normal human being?

My dearest diary, here is more information about Lynn and how she dealt with life's challenges, including her experiences with marijuana.

There were peer groups in high school—especially in sports, choir, or music. Lynn fit into the sports scene abroad, while I fit into the sports scene at my high school. Many times students are highly skilled with strong talents in other areas like computers, arts, and even business management. They are usually gifted in some areas and aren't influenced by peers. Lynn was especially gifted in sports but didn't fit into the high school system. She was an excellent artist with an eye for details. Her friends were limited. Each of us possessed a special mystery talent shrouded by deception. Lynn could outrun and outswim most of her peers. We could have competed in racing, and probably both of us would have won, competing against each other; however, I swim like a rock, while Lynn swims like a fish. She had hidden talents in art, photography, and writing skills that would bypass most other students. Yet she did not fit into the usual student lineup with the activities groups at her new high school. I was active in band and played on the tennis team for third doubles and then moved forward the next year to first singles. My senior year I received an award for tennis. Where was the award for Lynn's talents?

What happens when such a teenager goes through intense mood swings? What if she showed these very sad and silly times to her peers and they started talking behind her back? Luckily, growing up, I didn't have this pressure from peers. Perhaps part of this teenager's actions was due to a hidden bipolar disorder, something that was only recognized almost a half century later. Lynn liked being outspoken and funny even as a teenager. She liked being the life of the party because she wanted to be the center of attention.

She left home after high school graduation and found groups who smoked marijuana. This drug gave her highs, which led her to try out other drugs. For years she smoked thin cigarettes, and the black smoke she inhaled remained locked up in her lungs. Eventually, it got so bad she suffered from exhaustion and even had to use an inhaler at times. Eventually, she used alcohol along with drugs, living the wild life. Many years later a special man came into her life who loved and accepted her. For the first time in her life, she found true happiness. The past was the past, and she moved forward.

This marriage vow was the true love of her life. She was married to her superman for more than twenty years. This marriage lasted because the love to honor vows outweighed the choice of divorce and the loneliness divorce could bring. The man became Lynn's hero for staying with her during her ups and downs, including many DUIs that often landed her in jail for several months.

What would a normal life really be like for her? After all the years with ups and downs, highs and lows, could she adjust to a normal life after her parents passed away? She sought out peace. What a challenge for her bipolar disorder. The worst was the past challenge of watching her mother decline from a beautiful and caring mother into someone she didn't know or couldn't even identify.

How could I encourage Lynn to see brighter days in her future? I felt like she sometimes looked at me as her counselor or psychologist.

I had no training and didn't want responsibility for giving advice. Thinking back, Lynn was educating me in a world I knew nothing about, and I learned how it influenced her sometimes, changing her life from past negative choices to joyful happy times.

Lynn spoke on the subject of marijuana. We were very open during so many conversations. I confessed to Lynn that once I was invited to a late-evening party. She was all ears. Meeting new single people who were in their early twenties was special to me because I wanted to expand and create new friendships. We listened to records from the late sixties. Laughter and great conversations from the moment I arrived thrilled my heart. Then they turned the lights down low, and everyone joined in a circle. I noticed people were quiet and smoking joints. When they handed it to me, I took it, looked at it, smelled it, and then made the choice to hand it off to the next person. People around the room looked at me. Minutes later I thanked the person who invited me and excused myself. Arriving home, I patted myself on the back and smiled in the mirror. To this day, I am very glad I made that major decision. Lynn's experiences with marijuana encouraged her to pursue different highs, and I realized I didn't need to hang out with the "in" crowd. I had made a good choice. Of course, I wasn't invited to any more parties.

Over the past several years, I have heard the pros and cons about marijuana. I have seen states pass marijuana laws making it legal for businesses to sell it in various forms. But I listened to a marijuana user named Lynn. This is what she told me about this substance.

Marijuana has loads of other names—pot, dope, grass, weed, and some others. It is easily grown and smoked. The plant has a chemical that can make a person feel high. For Lynn's bad back, it helped relieve some of the pain. It also caused her to hallucinate sometimes. Lynn informed me that marijuana can be laced with other drugs that will cause bad reactions. Most importantly, Lynn spoke about the results of inhaling the smoke. The ingredients were carried into her lungs and bloodstream, impairing the respiratory system. According to Lynn, marijuana led her to experiment with other harder drugs in order to get even higher.

I personally believe it's likely bad for a person's health, and I've gathered that even with the small knowledge about marijuana. I have concluded that this drug might affect a person's brain and body just like it did Lynn's. By the time Lynn realized what had happened to her mind and body, it would be too late because it stayed in her bloodstream. To this day, I can smell marijuana on people as they walk near me. Sometimes the smell lingers in their clothes and hair.

With marijuana, Lynn and other people may be put at risk with bad judgment calls. They may get high and decide to drive a car. Lynn felt anxious when she was high and realized she had slower coordination and reaction time, which could have led to a car accident and injuries. She was very lucky not to have had any accidents, only DUIs. Perhaps some people have no desire to advance to new highs. Every person's body is different.

I've watched TV shows about the positive side of marijuana. It is good to hear both sides because the other side speaks about how and when a drug can help in positive ways. It's worth smoking or taking that drug when people have been helped with their pains. I have not heard of one person who has abused marijuana when they use it for medicinal purposes. More power to them.

Lynn loved to talk about herself. She said, "I've paid the price for bad choices."

An email presented her confession. Reading the email brought a smile on my face. My precious, dearest diary, I'm so glad to show you how much life meant to Lynn. The future was bright as she moved forward. It was like the sun coming over the hillside and blotting out the past mistakes. She was full of life.

Message dated 2/13/07 3:11 AM (Partial email)

Five DUI's! Quit drinking a year ago, but popped a valium here and there, with all this stress over my mom. It took forever but I finally got tired of hangovers, jail cells, revoked driver licenses, ignition interlocks, and just plan drinking. They hold no interest for me anymore. I just had enough of jails. Even the smell of whiskey makes me sick. I spent a year in jail without my mother bailing me out or even visiting me when I was nineteen years old. My mother disowned me and it was a time that I started to grow up. I spent my twentieth birthday in jail with no one visiting me. At the last minute she showed up at my trial, got on the stand and begged the judge to give me another chance, and he did. I got probation, so mom is not all that bad. She just was not thrilled that her daughter was in the county jail. It all worked out. Lynn

(When she wrote emails she was very direct.)

I told Lynn I admired her working as a bartender because she looked like she didn't encourage clients to drink too much. She bellowed with laughter, commenting that those drunks paid for so many of her drinks that driving home was called DUI time. Well, sometimes I can be wrong about a person.

She mentioned how she thought being jailed during her late teens helped her grow up. But to what degree did she grow up? Did she think she was infallible? Did she like the challenge of not getting caught? Perhaps it was her way to embarrass her parents for moving back to the United States, where she couldn't show off her talents.

My heart goes out to anyone who has a precious loved one in jail and those who are serving time. Some people just need to learn the hard way after incarceration. That person usually has a good heart but just kept walking on the wrong path for whatever reason. I really believe that people in jail don't realize what an impact their bad choices have had on parents, children, and relatives. These people in jail are not alone by any means. As for the person who makes excuses and won't admit to the wrong he or she has done, probably hurting so many people in the process, the individual can remain in jail so we on the outside are safe.

Lynn and I had conversations regarding retirement and where we would like to live. She mentioned that she loved living near the water. Perhaps they would move to Colorado or someplace where there was a lake and some farmland.

Then we conversed about great organizations that donate to hospitals and help people around the world. Lynn's eyes became bright just to think about helping other people. She was excited to talk about giving and helping, especially through educational scholarships, to young people reaching for their dreams or children in hospitals. Together, we came up with a few wonderful organizations like Rotary International, the Lions, Eagles, and Elks organizations, the Masons, and so many more caring organizations that help those less fortunate or provide disaster relief. Many of these organizations' scholarships are exceptionally well used by the recipients.

Another time when Lynn stopped by on a Sunday afternoon, her previous occupation came up. She didn't look in my eyes, so something was wrong. I took over and restated that her past life was past. To have been a bartender meant a person needed to be talented at working with people. As a bartender, she must have been a great listener, psychologist, protector, priest, and socializer who understood clients' secrets. She must have been friendly but not too open to become friends. As a bartender, she must have been alert, knowing exactly when to cut off clients without upsetting them. As a bartender she was highly respected because she remembered each client's face, name, and information. She would not look down or disrespect or even dismiss herself as an uncaring human being. In her job position, she might just have been the person who helped save a client from causing an accident. She should be proud of herself for having that authority.

It was Lynn who told me about the twelve AA steps (www.alcoholicsananymous.com).

Looking back, Lynn and I laughed at one of our Sunday conversations when we named peoples' character traits and attitudes. We agreed that both of us at some time in our lives had been part of each of the following listed words. I quickly grabbed a pencil and paper to write down our jokes.

- Kind, Mean, Rude, Bold, Anxious
- Funny, Smart, Happy, Brave, Educated
- Quiet, Noisy, Loves, Loyal, Talkative
- Laughs, Strong, Honest, Gloomy, Frightened
- Lively, Greedy, Daring, Poetic
- Hopeful, Playful, Jealous, Selfish
- Patient, Excited, Private, Carefree
- Helpless, Artistic, Athletic, Creative
- Outgoing, Friendly, Depressed, Observant
- Questioned, Sorrowful, Spiritual, Dependable
- Thoughtful, Challenged, Responsive, Determined
- Industrious, Trustworthy, Disobedient, Humorous
- Reliable, Kindhearted, Courageous, Confident

These were just a few words that were written down.

Lynn and I took some of the words and developed a word game. We named the game "Traits, Attitudes, and Beyond." We were amazed at how our life experiences brought out explaining a word because we were both wives, mothers, daughters, employees, and most importantly, women.

The "Traits, Attitudes, and Beyond" game had easy rules.

- Two or more players can participate.
- Write a word on a piece of paper describing attitudes and character traits.
- Make a pile of words.
- Place the words between players.
- Each player takes turns by picking up one of the written words.
- Each player says the word and then briefly details a life experience.

Examples
- Love: I love my husband and children.
- Loud: I play music very loud.
- Athletic: I can run and swim.
- Thoughtful: It was thoughtful of you to deliver flowers to my parents.

We had so much fun that the time together passed quickly. We never went into much detail about our lives. The game helped us to talk about her alcoholism and substance abuse. Each person is an individual with choices.

Chapter 15

Fighting Bipolar Disorder

My dearest diary, bipolar and Alzheimer's diseases are extremely emotional subjects for me to write about. There are many professionals who can comment on the different levels of coping strategies. I can only talk about what I noticed and experienced with Anita and Lynn plus what I have learned from the information I sought out.

The best book regarding bipolar disorder I have read is by author Kay Jamison. The book is titled *An Unquiet Mind: A Memoir of Moods and Madness*. The author is an American clinical psychologist and writer who focuses on bipolar disorder.

Every person has talents and skills they've developed with education and life experiences. As a bipolar personality, Lynn learned the hard way by being incarcerated and surviving life's experiences. It was hard for her to hold on to a job due to her personal drinking. Was it really her drinking, or could it have been the bipolar disorder that affected her mind and emotions? She had a good work ethic, but something kept pushing her over the edge.

Message Dated 3/1/07 10:18 AM (Partial email)

Everyone in my family went to college, but I went to jail—so what? I got my education in life, just living it, mistakes and all. I kept locating work, usually as a bartender because no one else would hire me. I made great tips! I am proud to tell you that I paid my bills, never lived on welfare because people poke their nose into my business, and finally learned my lesson serving in jail "several" times. I do not drink, smoke pot, or even shoplift anymore. I do take valium when needed, but no more drugs. Cold turkey—times done! When I was a bartender I drank a lot with all those drunks! I stole some money once bartending; felt so guilty the next day that I put the money back. Life was hard at times, stealing not acceptable, except food when hungry and clothes from those big owned stores to survive looking good. That was wrong too. Telling you too much. Love you for helping my mother. Your friend, Lynn.

Lynn knew which of her clients were big tippers. She was good at doing that math. She connected with customers and remembered their names, faces, and information, making each one personally feel special. But there was a very serious side of Lynn. She reached out to hurting people.

As for me, I could not understand Lynn being depressed since she usually appeared upbeat and happy when we saw each other in person. But I saw the opposite coming through her emails. In the past I would simply have had no further contact with such a person who could not function the way I expected. Was I judgmental? Yes, it was my choice to make sure my life did not include people like Lynn. I didn't understand that she just wanted to be accepted for who she was. I had my own issues with Lynn; however, over time we started to trust each other's opinions and experiences.

Accepting Lynn gave a whole new meaning to my life experiences. This new learning experience opened up new doors of understanding. I noticed how Lynn loved to laugh at life. She didn't want to show the world her painful experiences. Because of Lynn's two different sides with her bouts of joy and anger, our growing friendship stalled in the mud.

Bipolar depression needs to be treated. Otherwise, the person can become suicidal. I found this out too late. Most of Lynn's life was self-sabotaged. She mentioned ordering medications from other countries. She never really knew what was in them, only that she thought the drugs helped her maintain her *sanity*.

By studying some information on bipolar depression, I now have a clearer understanding what she meant by the word sanity. I blame myself for not being more understanding and patient with my friend. God is very merciful.

Learning about the symptoms of bipolar depression after Lynn passed away was exhausting. As I read and gained a little bit of knowledge, her actions started to make more sense.

I remember her email telling me that the "music just stopped" and that she could "feel nothing." It did not bother me because Lynn was always telling me how she felt. I should have been a much better friend and realized she was really seeking help in the only way she knew how. She was such a moody person.

So what is bipolar disorder? I found it to be a serious brain illness. There are highs and lows where people can't control their emotions. The highs are called mania, and the lows are called depression.

According to the National Institute of Mental Health, bipolar disorder can be treated. I was surprised to read that family genes often pass on the disorder through the development of abnormal brain structure and functioning. Did Anita have bipolar disorder? I also read about anxiety disorders. This was really heavy information. My life was so simple compared to Lynn's struggle for daily survival.

There was a brochure that mentioned basic things to do. I only scribbled down some notes, and I'm not sure if the order is correct.

1) Be patient. (I was not patient with Lynn.)
2) Encourage the person to talk. Listen carefully. (Okay, this I did.)
3) Be understanding of moods. (Forget this one.)
4) Help your friend have fun. (We did that most of the time, laughing at ourselves.)

5) Help your friend understand there is treatment. (I did not know anything about this at all. However, Lynn said she kept in contact with her doctor about her lungs and back.)

Another site helped me gain a clearer understanding how Lynn must have lived. I learned there is a category of mood disorders that is defined by the presence of one or more episodes of abnormally elevated energy levels, cognition, and moods that can cause depression. I was surprised to learn there are several levels of bipolar disorder.

Then I returned to Maslow's *Hierarchy of Needs*.

The missing links for Lynn appeared to be success with an educational degree and her self-esteem dealing with her parents. She was very intelligent, but past choices kept her trapped. She seldom let go of the things she knew were bad for her. As we would talk, I wondered why she was entrusting me with her past. Was her subconscious coming out? I never felt sorry for her because it was her life. We spoke about our lives and what we would have changed if we had known then what we experienced during our lifetime. We agreed to disagree.

We agreed that if we had changed the past, we would have received our PhDs and hung them on our business walls. Somehow education still was very much a part of our self-esteem and confidence. Sure, we joked around, but the real hidden subconscious told both of us that the path we had taken wasn't the path we really wanted out of life since we both put value on education.

There is more information that I could relay to you, but some conversations should remain silent even to you, my dearest diary. Sometimes as Lynn would say, "It is nobody's business but mine."

Chapter 16

Alzheimer's Disease and Health Concerns

Looking back upon Anita, Lynn, and our embracing hearts we became all entwined together. Anita had prayed for another daughter. Lynn wanted to be loved and free to be a real wife. And as for me, I just said yes to making a phone call for books.

Over those couple of years, the entwined hearts gradually united the three of us so that we could become one heart filled with love and forgiveness most of the time. God does answer prayers. It just takes Him time to place all the puzzle pieces together.

It was Alzheimer's that forged a common cord connecting Anita, Lynn, and me. Anita had Alzheimer's. Lynn was the daughter who watched over her ill mother. I hope I was the person who helped build a forgiving bridge between mother and daughter.

I remember that my uncle had Alzheimer's. According to my cousin, he did not recognize anyone and slithered away in the night after he was diagnosed six months earlier. He had lived a very active and full life as a farmer. He drank wine now and then and took care of his eating habits, mostly with foods grown from the garden. He held normal conversations and enjoyed people, and he was strong and healthy all of his life except the last six months. Suddenly, his mind quickly faded away.

A neighbor's father had Alzheimer's. We knew each other about eight years. There were times when she just needed to come over and have some coffee. She talked about traveling someday. She spoke very little about the stress of Alzheimer's, but her face consistently showed what she did not say.

Alzheimer's disease is a degenerative disorder affecting the brain and causing dementia. It is a slow-progressing type of dementia caused by a gradual loss of a person's brain cells. It usually starts with the disruption of nerve cells dealing with communication skills and metabolism. As the nerve cells become more and more damaged, the cells eventually die. During this time period, the memory fails, a person's personality changes, and daily activities become impossible to perform.

Presently, there are no cures. However, many organizations are striving to locate a solution.

A healthy diet, exercise, and weight management can help protect against Alzheimer's; however, this was exactly what Anita's life was like. She produced her own garden with delicious vegetables. She had apple and orange trees. Anita knew exactly how to use spices and created her own desserts. She ate fish at least once a week and drank water often. Yet how did a very healthy and active lady obtain this horrible disease?

Over time Alzheimer's was starting to get me down emotionally, seeing Anita fade.

There are supports groups that can help family members cope with the stress of dealing with Alzheimer's. I could not understand why Lynn wanted to walk this walk alone. Why did she not seek out a local group that specialized in this subject where she could have spoken and asked questions? They could have been there to help her realize she was not alone? Each family member handled the situation in their own way. It was none of my business.

Then I remembered that Lynn did not like groups because of the many years of attending AA meetings. She thought the Alzheimer's support group could not help her either. Some wishes do not come into existence, and that was her choice.

I found there are many places online to find out more information about Alzheimer's. Perhaps this is what Lynn did to

JJ Janice

fill in her expectations to gain knowledge about Alzheimer's. I still feel so uninformed even after gaining additional knowledge by exploring the different websites and learning more about the different stages.

Alzheimer's disease loves to attack people of all walks of life. All people are ordinary human beings when it comes to Alzheimer's.

I have searched several websites for the signs of Alzheimer's. (See www.stagesofalzheimer'sdisease.com and http://alothealth.com/conditions/stages-of-alzheimers-disease-5840.) What great information. These websites are informational and to the point.

Stages of Alzheimer's Disease (partial information list)

Stage 1: Patient's cognition area is not yet affected.

Stage 2: Cognitive ability declines in mild ways (e.g., misplaced keys, not recalling names of acquaintances, forgetting dates).

Stage 3: Symptoms are still fairly subtle. A doctor might be able to diagnose at this point. People will begin to repeat themselves frequently, unable to perform tasks at home or on the job. They will have difficulty with organization, and they will be unable to develop new skills. This stage lasts two to three years.

Stage 4: Now the patient is accurately diagnosed. Cognitive decline affects the person's ability to do everyday tasks at home like dressing or preparing meals. Emotional changes occur because of moodiness and confusion, and the person is unable to live on his or her own. Average time length for this stage is two years.

Stage 5: Patient no longer lives alone. Disease progressed to difficulty recalling memories such as birthdays, addresses, current day of the week, or even weather conditions.

Stage 6: Patients lose ability to perform most basic functions, including taking a bath or going to the bathroom. They might confuse seeing people regularly visiting them and even forget people entirely. These patients will become more afraid and angry, and they are difficult to console.

Stage 7: Patients will need continual supervision and assistance in order to survive on a daily basis. The speech function gradually diminishes so they can eventually only respond with one or two words. By the end of this stage, the patients are unable to walk, stand, or sit without support. The average life span is one and a half years. Death is commonly the result of pneumonia.

So what is pneumonia? I searched and searched for a better understanding and located just the right website, www.NorthwestPrimeTime.com (Gloria May, "Understanding Pneumonia," *Northwest Prime Time*, October 2010). Here are some basic facts about pneumonia. It is an inflammatory condition of one or both lungs. It can affect any age, and it is caused by bacteria or a virus irritating the air sacs in the lungs, which then fill with fluid. This interferes with the lungs' ability to deliver oxygen to the blood and remove carbon dioxide. The person usually coughs up greenish or yellowish sputum or blood, and the illness produces shortness of breath, chills, weakness, and fatigue.

I have penned this information to you, my dearest diary, because I needed to let my thoughts out about subjects that I know very little about. Thank you for listening to me, and I know you will not criticize or judge me. I love you.

Chapter 17

Everyone Is Human

The paths of life can connect different types of people in unity. Your past does not matter. How much money you have, the title you hold, the way you dress, the way you speak, or even the place you live—none of that matters in the afterlife. However, I have now learned there are really two different types of people—the common (Lynn and me) who live simple lives and the public figures (Anita and Tom) whose names and influences expand beyond the community to an outer world.

Many of life's illnesses claim both groups of people. Everyone is a human being with personal needs. Each person is connected to a family. Anita and Tom had friends to joke with, cry and laugh with, shop for food and clothes with, and enjoy vacationing with. Most people in each group have bank accounts and enjoy hobbies of some sort. The common and public figures like taking day trips, reading, eating at fast-food places and nice restaurants. Both types want to be remembered, especially by their families.

The difference could be the flashing of cameras. Those who are common like to take pictures of their families and special events. Many times pictures are shown to family members, relatives, neighbors, coworkers, even people we don't know that well. The difference could be that public figures might prefer to have their pictures taken by professionals who showcase their community involvement or travels in the newspapers or magazines.

Common people can drive in public and choose a restaurant without being noticed. The only signature required of us is the one for the bill. On the contrary, the public figure might enjoy an evening out with family or friends only to be interrupted and asked to place an autograph on a picture or a menu. Maybe it would include a selfie? I don't know if this happened to Anita, but Lynn reported, "My mother no longer makes public appearances." I smiled and chuckled, remembering a very funny experience that I mentioned to Lynn. "I was walking inside a grocery store, and a lady stopped, looked at my face, smiled, and congratulated me. My picture was in a local newspaper as Employee of the Month. It was a funny feeling because I was just a common person who cared about each student." Lynn remained silent.

Both groups are polite in public; however, the actual public becomes a silent factor that perhaps helps determine the public figure's daily activities in the public.

Lynn mentioned that there were times when her parents were on an assignment and would stop at a vacation spot only to be noticed by an excited commoner because of a magazine article. The result was then that there was no privacy. If something happened to the family (e.g., Lynn going to jail because of marijuana or too many DUIs), it might be considered a reflection on what had happened inside their home. People might have seen her parents as bad influences when it was really a wild child growing into adulthood. How could this family even try to explain that their grown-up child had chosen to make bad choices? They couldn't. It's the family's conversations and love that will eventually determine the wild child's future outcome and help him or her change into a better person. Of course, there are those tabloids that don't say if something is true or not. Some magazines and newspapers just want people to pay and gossip. Is this what Anita found out?

The common people are ordinary people who want to be ordinary, but so do those who are in the limelight. Everyone has their own interests, talents, and abilities. I will always remember the time Anita and Tom asked me what money meant to me. It is how we gain and use the money that is really important. But having money makes life so much easier when it's used for good. Having extra money offered Anita and Tom the opportunity to build a better life.

The furniture in anyone's apartment or home depends on choices. Us three ladies enjoyed furniture that did not need to be totally matched. We liked furniture especially made by skilled hands showing an individual's talents. As for Lynn, she mentioned one day she was going to purchase all matching furniture. There are all types of people who have immaculate homes where everything matches. Some of these homes are actually houses where people live, while others are homes where people love to belong. Mine is not one of those perfect homes; it is a home where you don't need to phone in advance because coffee or tea can always be made within minutes to maximize laughter and conversations. Anita and Tom's home was a home to me. Thank you.

Anita once commented that every person has talents, skills, joys, and sorrows. Everyone has responsibilities that ensure everything flows smoothly on a daily basis. Every person has some type of title. Anita loved being called Mom. My dearest diary, the word *mom* has so much responsibility connected to it. Moms are loving. We must offer a shoulder for strength or disciple and encourage. We shop for groceries, cook, tend to injuries, serve as the family accountant, clean up the spills, clean the house, drive everyone around—the list can go on and on. Mom wears a lot of hats. This can apply to dads too. It does not matter what walk of life a person is born into. People are people, and each person has responsibilities. But most important is the ability to forgive and receive love.

We all need a supportive shoulder. It doesn't matter if a person comes from a family of common or public figures. Perhaps it is good to remind oneself that a family is just a family. But what is important is for a family to be happy together. But what happens when someone becomes ill in the family? When it comes to Alzheimer's, there are no distinctions about who is who.

Any family member going through Alzheimer's is not alone. Here is a list of a few famous people who were just ordinary people going through the various stages of Alzheimer's. Maybe you recognize the names or know of additional casualties. Do you think their stardom made their family's stress any different from a common family whose loved one ended up with Alzheimer's?

- Malcom Young, legendary guitarist
- Glen Campbell, country singer and guitarist
- Pat Summit, coach of the Tennessee Lady Vols basketball team
- Perry Como, popular singer and television personality
- Charles Bronson, star in numerous action films
- Ronald Reagan, fortieth US president and actor
- Charlton Heston, actor, legacy of entertainment contributions
- Norman Rockwell, famous American painter
- Rita Hayworth, American film star
- Sugar Ray Robinson, boxer
- Aaron Copeland, renowned classical composer
- Burgess Meredith, TV actor
- Estelle Getty, TV actress
- Peter Falk, TV actor

Nuns, priests, the elderly, young, middle-aged, firemen, teachers, bookkeepers, carpenters, policemen, businesspeople, moms and dads, sisters and brothers—name the occupation or relative or friend, and you'll see how Alzheimer's seeks and reaches out to everyone. It does not discriminate.

I will not write about the percentages because numbers constantly change. However, I will tell you how Alzheimer's disease received its name.

Alzheimer's disease is named after Dr. Alois Alzheimer, German neuropathologist and clinician. He first discovered this disease in 1907 while examining Frau Auguste D.'s autopsy (see *The Everything Alzheimer's Book*).

What causes Alzheimer's is unknown. Many have speculated, but nothing is truly definitive at this point. There are many organizations doing research. Each area of the brain is being explored, and new information is constantly being found with updates sent out from the various organizations to the public, especially through various health magazines. There is a huge challenge to find the truth about what causes Alzheimer's. Working together is essential.

Every person has a purpose, no matter who they are and what their title. I only wish people could read what I'm writing about Anita and Lynn so that their purpose could include showing others that our experiences are all part of being human.

Thank you, my dearest diary. Now walk with my thoughts as I view rooms in order to close each door to my two-year life experience with my entwined ladies. It was a very special time for closure.

Chapter 18

The Closing Doors

My dearest diary, there comes a time to say goodbye to parts of our past. Time flew by, and before realizing how time controlled my life, I was ready to close the chapter on the past. These moments show up at the oddest times.

When my mother sold our family farm after dad passed away, I wanted to take a last look around. The home had turned into an empty house. My mother said I couldn't. I inquired about a children's book about Frederick Douglass. It was my only book growing up—except for the Bible. Mom mentioned that everything had been cleaned out as far as she knew and the book had probably been tossed into a bonfire. I asked if she recalled the outside cover. It was green with the word *Freddy* on it. It was a book of encouragement that all things are possible. Again, my mother repeated she probably burned it or threw it away because all the rooms were now empty. I never again questioned my mother. My heart sank because this book had meant so much to me that I had hid it up in the attic to protect it. It was so deeply disappointing when I realized that she had not listened to how much that simple book meant to me. If only I had been allowed to check in the attic one last time to see if the hidden place still had that precious book.

I viewed the outside of the house, which once was a home. My memory raced back to when I was seven years old and we moved into this old, remodeled farmhouse. I was excited by the running water that didn't need to be pumped and that white electric stove, which replaced the old wood stove in the rental farm home. That indoor bathroom had a real bathtub with running hot water. It was so exciting. This new two-bedroom home with the bathroom sure did beat walking to the outhouse no matter the weather or time of day. Once I opened that outhouse door, and I saw (and smelled) a skunk passing by. That memory is still fresh in my mind and nostrils. A skunk's smell is something a person never forgets.

I recalled when my mother did the wash. Our laundry was cleaned with the newly purchased washing machine. We still needed to hang the clothes up on the clothesline to dry in the fresh air. Our family was moving up in the world.

I lived in this home from second grade through high school, and I returned to it during college years. It was around as I advanced in the workforce, married, and had children. When my mother chose to sell our home, I observed her slowly using the pitchfork to stoke the fire, which she had filled with wood from the bulldozed garage. What an empty space. Then my sister and I encouraged our mother to say goodbye to the farm where she had lived in for half of a century. It was very hard for her to leave that home. Thinking back, she didn't look back or turn her head as we drove off to the newly purchased retirement apartment at the senior estates community.

Several years later I drove past our old farm and realized only a small amount of the driveway appeared. The new owners had torn down the one-hundred-plus-year-old farmhouse, the three old chicken barns, and even the old apple tree I would climb for the best tasting apples. Those two thousand chickens had supplied eggs to several country stores in the neighborhood. I was taught to reach under even old hens and gather eggs, sort the eggs, and make sure each egg was cleaned. Who would want to purchase a dirty egg? These were just daily responsibilities as I was taught the value of working. I missed looking at the barn door where I learned to hit a solid tennis ball. Of course, the ground was dirt with gravel, and that ball would travel in whatever direction it wanted. As a result, playing on a tennis court with smooth cement was so easy on my feet.

My mind retreated back to the olden days and how our mom would stoke bonfires with a pitch fork to burn the weekly trash. I remembered running around the two-acre berry fields and timing myself. Sometimes I would sit down in one of the boysenberry rows just to be by myself. My dearest diary, if you were real, where would you go just to be alone? I know people who go to the restroom just to release their stress and read a newspaper. There were just some things that brought out wonderful memories.

At that time I had not met Lynn. I later found out she loved to race too. When we're in heaven, perhaps we'll find a race track around a football field, and I can challenge Lynn to see who is faster. And then there might be a tennis court where I can challenge Anita to a great tennis game. Both games would sell out, I'm sure. Maybe in heaven we have great muscles and fast legs like when we were young. Isn't earth a duplicate of heaven?

The new owners replaced all those buildings with trees. Even the seven-acre wheat field and garden area no longer existed. Our old farmhouse with the beautiful snowball tree was gone. I searched for pictures of our farmhouse, but I only found a few. I was so happy that my sister took a picture of the old homestead and an artist created a picture for each season. What a great memory gift. Thank you for the memories.

I wondered why Lynn and I had not spoken much about growing up and where we lived. I knew she traveled and lived with her parents in many different countries. As for me, I am glad to say that I attended a two-room schoolhouse from second through eighth grade. Sadly, if we had moved to the farm a year earlier, I could have told Lynn I attended a one-room schoolhouse, moved into a two-room schoolhouse, and then advanced into high school. People nowadays don't even understand what I'm talking about. *What is an outhouse?* Perhaps the reason we didn't speak very much about our growing up days was because we were focused on her mother, my mentor.

Now was the time to come back to reality. It was exactly that time again to say goodbye to this warm home in my heart, but would this family allow me to view each room in my mind? Would they allow me to do this final walk? It was their home, but how I loved that peacefulness each time I entered this special home. It taught me it was okay to love someone other than my family. How could I ask this fabulous family to allow me the privilege to view each room and say goodbye?

Tom closed his eyes. Several hours passed by, and finally, people led Tom from the home to a van. Suddenly, everything changed. A family member asked the caregiver and me to help locate live flowers throughout the home because it would be closed up once everyone departed. I really appreciated this individual's wonderful, caring heart. I had seen it several times at the convalescent center and other get-togethers. I started to walk with them when I dropped into my own world of memory. This was the answer to the prayer that I could view each room and have a few moments alone.

Walking down the hallway to Anita's bedroom, my eyes glanced at the various happy family pictures. These must have been much happier times for everyone. Entering Anita's room, I saw that silver sweater still folded on the dresser. I reached out, picked up the sweater, dipped my head into the sweater, and smelled Anita's scent. Then I hugged it to my chest. I appreciated this private moment to reflect on her beauty. Next, I very carefully refolded it. Glancing around the room, I realized all the little things were no longer on the queen-size bed. Lynn must have taken them with her several months earlier. I closed my eyes, took a deep breath, and realized my eyes were filling up with tears. I put my head up, shoulders back, and immediately left the room, not returning to view it.

Tom's room was empty. It was the second time that day I had entered his room. How funny the way the mind works. There was a huge bay window in this room too! Somehow I had never noticed this before, not even when saying goodbye to Tom a few hours earlier. I whispered again, "Thank you, Tom, for allowing me to enter your peaceful home and visit with your beautiful wife and you over the past two years." I wanted to cry, but I put my shoulders back and kept my head up. I needed to be strong.

I walked down the short hallway, viewing the many family pictures on what I called the family picture wall. Lynn had taken so many pictures. My thoughts raced, thinking how creative she was and what a special eye for photography she had.

I turned right to enter the bathroom, but why? I noticed two empty spots were outlined by the mirror and sink areas. The previous two needlepoints on the wall had faded the wall's color. Then I felt like Lynn and Anita were right next to me. My right elbow moved out as if someone was holding on to it. My mind returned to the place where Lynn had made those needlepoint designs. One was the Lord's Prayer (Matthew 6:9–13).

The Lord's Prayer

Our Father which art in heaven, Hallowed be Thy name.

Thy kingdom come, Thy will be done in earth, as it is in heaven.

Give us this day our daily bread. And forgive us our debts, as we forgive our debtors.

And lead us not into temptation, but deliver us from evil:

For Thine is the kingdom, and the power, and the glory.

Forever. Amen.

How many times had Anita read these words as she gazed upon this handmade gift by the bathroom mirror? When Lynn had taken down the two tapestries the day of the cremation, I saw that dust on top of both frames had gathered throughout the years. My tapestry was a simple poem. I told you about it earlier while penning chapter 11. Many times as I read over these words, my heart has said,

JJ Janice

"Thank you again for allowing me in your family home and passing on to me this beautiful saying to be hung on my dining room wall."

My ears heard Anita's heavenly laughter as I entered the small TV room. My memory noticed Tom enjoying Carmen. There were no more beads of sweat dripping from my brow, moving so many heavy boxes of books. Tom no longer said, "Hi there," as I entered his entertainment room. There was no more asking Tom what he would enjoy eating when I returned to visit him. I looked at my arm, and there was no soft hand touching my sleeve. It flashed in my mind that the last time I had spoken with Tom, we looked into each other's eyes. As I was about to say goodbye, instead I blurted out, "I love you, Papa." Where had that come from? We just stared at each other. Then Tom smiled that family smile, and tears formed in both of our eyes. I immediately needed to leave.

That day driving home, I could actually hear Lynn say, "Thank you for telling my Papa that I love him." I felt so good inside. Can people actually communicate from the beyond? Okay, my dearest diary, I am glad you are not real, and I can honestly pen you. If you were real, you would probably think I was a bit loopy.

There was the back door that Tom's wheelchair barely fit through. One could park the car along a paved path met and pick up Tom to take him to the doctor and other appointments. I smiled and even started to giggle a little remembering Anita showing me the back way downstairs. The caregiver and I were trying to catch up with Anita so she would not fall down the steep stairs. What a fabulous day that was, asking Anita to be our guest author. As for Lynn, stepping down those stairs was a time for her to show me all that paperwork we needed to clean up. Before walking back upstairs, I stopped and took a deep breath. Looking up, I noticed no one had taken down the large picture of Anita standing near the huge swordfish that had taken her hours to reel in on one of those world travel adventures. What a very special time in her life. Those stairs really were steep.

But first, I took one last look, viewing the many bookshelves still all cleared off and remembering all those wonderful books now safe in my basement. The broken mirror was still on the wall. That was the mirror that I thought was too large for me to take home. That mirror was larger than my car. In fact, it was as large as the bay window. There were so many papers on shelves on the opposite wall compared with the caregiver's area, which was nice, tidy, clean, and orderly. Was this the messy area where Lynn had located her mother's two brown bags filled with positive and negative notes about Lynn's life? I thought that if Anita wrote little thoughts about Lynn, perhaps she started one about me. Well, it would be interesting to read her thoughts about this common stranger. Gladly, Anita had lost her writing ability! Like before, I just closed my eyes for a few seconds, took some deep breaths, and turned toward the back basement door leading outside.

Looking through the basement window, I saw my car, which Anita had climbed into without any physical problems. It was that same car I used to carry away her precious boxes of books. I remember her thin arm stretched out with her feeble hand touching those books. How often had I arrived to visit, opened up the driver's door, looked up, waved back to Tom, and watched Anita slowly walk across the room to open their front door? I opened my eyes again. Now it seemed strange to see several cars parked in the driveway.

It was time to climb up the steep stairs one last time to check if there were any flowers elsewhere. By the way, what happened to the two ladies who were looking for flowers? Entering the kitchen, I saw the counter space spanning from the patio wall to the opposite wall, where the washer and dryer were located. The cupboard was fabulously spacious. Twelve people could easily be in that kitchen at one time all preparing food without bumping into one another. My eyes noticed the empty kitchen table where Tom, the caregiver, and I had eaten those tasty hamburgers and fries together. Tom looked so happy that day.

My attention was brought back to the family talking together by the dining room table. The space was open between the kitchen and dining room. So many happy and serious conversations must have taken place over the many years of living here.

Sitting at the hand-carved living room table with Lynn must have always provided interesting conversations. My mind glanced back to the kitchen area, remembering Lynn taking all of her mother's cookbooks and passing them onto me. "I know my mother would want you to have them," I could hear Lynn saying as she smiled. This was a vitally important room because it must have witnessed many joyful times with family and friends as they sat at the kitchen table going through the various fishing cookbooks and enjoying happy conversations. My memory continued to close the chapter on each room. This was important because I felt walking through this wonderful warm home was the closure that I had not received at my old childhood home.

My mind returned to the family talking about the large prayer plant or Christmas cactus. It was more than fifty years old and trimmed back so the arms would not reach out toward the dining room table. No one had a place for this plant, so after some conversation, I agreed to take it home. It is still alive, and twice a year large pink flowers bloom in the living room. What a relaxing place this dining room area must have been when family and friends gathered for delightful conversations over the years, sitting together, enjoying some fondue looking over the lake, watching people relaxing while fishing from their boats. When I need a moment of relaxation, I just close my eyes and pretend to look out that dining room front window. It only exists in my memory now.

As we were all leaving the house, I glanced back and viewed the special family room. I remembered meeting Anita for the first time and later receiving her books. Then I returned for more books and saw love sparkle between Tom and Anita. I remembered walking back into this room after saying goodbye to this couple and the various times asking permission to give my regards to Tom in his TV room. So many times Anita looked directly into my eyes.

"I have been waiting for you," Anita had said several times as she greeted me by the front door and when we would walk together back to the living room. My mind swirled with warm memories. I thanked God Almighty for our paths crossing for a short season. I wondered who had said no to God when they had been asked to be this answer to Anita's prayer. It was scary at times, but it was fabulous that I had been chosen and was included in this wonderful private family. The memory path had turned into a cement road. I still feel honored to have been part of Anita's dream come true.

As the front door closed, I slowly walked down the three levels of steps one step at a time. I knew it would be the last time I would view the beautiful landscape and glance at the many cars. I carefully continued to walk down the rest of the front steps leading to the pavement. That special prayer plant needed to be protected from the overgrown shrubbery on the sides of the steps. Those overgrown plants had almost knocked Lynn and me down a year earlier as we walked arm in arm up these same steps.

Then at the bottom of the steps, I noticed a twig of Tom's plant seeking sunlight squeezed between two large shrubs. I had asked Tom if I could have a start of it, but I had never taken the time to tell him that I didn't know how to get a start of a plant. I didn't want him to know I was so ignorant! I do not even know that flower's name or the type of plant. The plant had a beautiful purple flower that spread out. Then the plant had a beautiful purple flower that eventually transformed into a see-through glaze. Being squeezed between these two other shrubs, I figured that plant eventually would be snuffed out. I hoped whoever purchased this house would find this special plant and give it new life. I realized the new owners would not have any emotional ties to the past owners' plants just like at my mother's home.

Backing out of the driveway, I looked up to the deck located above the double garage. Tears came to my eyes. Just a few weeks early, the family had met on that same deck for Lynn's passing. Only five days has passed since the family had gathered together and enjoyed some Peruvian food. The family must have had so many wonderful outings on that deck. Then my mind started to become creative as I pretended to see Tom and Anita holding each other in their arms and perhaps dancing to some twenties or thirties big band music along with Lynn playing a tambourine.

JJ Janice

I waved goodbye to this wonderful home. How I wanted to tell these family members that it had been a privilege to have met everyone. It was so important for me to view each room with happy memories. I had my closure. Unlike my mother's farm, this time I had permission to enter each room and say my farewells. I knew I would never see this wonderful family home again except in my memories. It was a home, not just a house.

People live in homes that are filled with welcome signs and the strong presence of flowing love. People can live in a home no matter where it is or what size it is because love overshadows everything, including harsh words.

How can I tell you, my dearest diary, your time spent with me has been very special? If you were real, we could go out to lunch. Of course, each of us would pay for our own meal, have some laughs, and talk together about our journeys in life. Those paths can be very dusty at times, yet always remember that there is sunlight high in the sky above the clouds!

God is a very merciful God who loves each of us with compassion. He holds His hand out to walk with us and carries us during stormy times in our lives too. It's good to trust God through these frustrating and worrisome times, but for me it was very hard because I'm not always so patient. Only God understands the future, placing paths together at the perfect time. He allowed me to go through this lightning storm so that I could build character, but in this situation right now, I'm not experiencing much positive character. I have been forcing my thoughts to be positive. Time will reveal His purpose and tell us how all the puzzle pieces fit together into each season.

Thank you, my dearest diary, again for being there for me as I have penned this story. It would have been very special if you had been real; however, best you are my imaginary friend. You have quietly witnessed the positive growth in my character. If you were real, maybe you could tell me your special seasons when God helped you through some tough times. What encouraging times these would be for both of us. Maybe our deep hurts would heal just from writing to each other. Since you are fictitious, I will print off these pages and hold you close to my heart.

In closing, consider perhaps the most important email from Lynn when she realized that she was remembered as she was going through the devastation of her mother's Alzheimer's. It's such an insensitive intruder! Yet at the very end of Alzheimer's, this intruder could not stop a dying mother from telling her precious daughter, "I love you." As for Lynn, I learned to accept people for who they are and not to live in a safe zone.

Message dated 1/16/07 9:41 AM (partial email)

Nobody should have to live like this. It is terribly depressing. I do not know how much more I can take. It is making me crazy. I LOVE MY BEAR! The homemade quilts are gorgeous also. It touched my heart when you said they were for "people who were hurting." Yes, I am hurting. I have to go to work. I believe I will strap my bear into the passenger seat and he can ride with me. I need a name. I am working on it. I will make a "him" or a "her." It will come to me eventually. By the way, I rode home with my new teddy bear on my lap. I used to make fun of adults and their bears… This is crazy?

My mother never wanted to live like this. I have lung problems from all my stupid years of smoking. I cannot afford an infection with my new tattoo. What do I do? I feel so lost at times. Getting my father to see mom is actually a major hassle for me. I have a very bad back. I was so relieved when he told me yesterday, "We do not need to do this every week." It is terribly depressing. Lynn

Thank you for listening to my story.

Love,
JJ

Resources

Alcoholism

- www.alcoholicsanonymous.com
- www.crchealth.com

Alzheimer's Disease

- Carolyn Dean, MD, *The Everything Alzheimer's Book* (Avon, MA: Adams Media, 2004), part of The Everything Series, xi and 1
- www.stagesofalzheimer's disease.com
- www.exlonpatch.com/into/diagnozing_treatment_alzheimers _dementia
- info@alz.org
- http/alothealth.com/conditions/stages-of-alzheimers-disease-5840

Bipolar Disorder

- www.facingbipolar.com
- www.enwikipedia.org/wiki/bipolar
- www.seroquelzr.com/bipolar-depression-systems
- • www.kayjamison.com

Cancer

- www.cancer.org

Heart

- www.americanheart.org
- www.fed.gov

Marijuana

- office@marijuana-anomymous.org
- www.marijuana-as-medicine.org/alliance.htm

Mental Health

- • www.mentalhealth.com
- • www.maslowshierarchyofneeds.com

Pneumonia

- www.NorthwestPrimeTime.com
- Gloria May, "Understanding Pneumonia," *Northwest Prime Time* (October 2010), 11

And the list could go on and on and on. Seek, and you will find. Knock, and the doors will open. You can gain this knowledge.

www.ingramcontent.com/pod-product-compliance
Lightning Source LLC
LaVergne TN
LVHW091547060526
838200LV00036B/739